Emperor of Mars

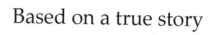

Based on a true story

Emperor of Mars

Jim Makichuk

Badland Publishing
Sherman Oaks, California

ISBN-10: 1466449772

ISBN-13: 978-1466449770

Library of Congress Control Number: 2011918993

Printed in the United States of America

Badland Publishing
Sherman Oaks, California

For Shirley, my 6th grade teacher

1

"Greetings, People of Earth," the voice said.

The final light of day glowed in warm orange tones across the horizon as the oncoming darkness spread over the flat lands of the Midwest. A bright star, just to the right of Venus, sparkled. It was Mars. Far beneath it, on a small patch of Earth stood two grain elevators that towered at the end of Main Street which ran down the middle of the sleeping town of Empire. The tall elevators stood like silent sentinels against the deep blue sky which would soon be dark. Beyond the town, a flat-topped mountain loomed along the horizon. Dark clouds spread over the mountain and distant thunder accompanied a flash of lightning.

Empire was like a thousand other little towns that dotted the flat prairie land that stretched across the middle of the continent. It was built along the railroad lines that ran from the Atlantic Ocean to the Pacific. This was farm land; mostly wheat grew around Empire, golden sheaves that swayed in the wind like ocean waves. The towns usually had anywhere from four hundred to a thousand people who lived in them and maybe another few hundred who lived on the farms nearby.

This town was somewhere in the middle with its five hundred and sixty-eight towners, as the farmers called them. Not much happened in Empire, the big cities had all the excitement. But if it was your home, you would have the same things anyone else did anywhere. You'd have parents, a house, friends, dogs, cats, you'd ride bicycles, you'd play cowboys and you would sometimes just marvel at the incredible sunsets that graced the flat lands around you.

It was October, in a time not so long ago that most people would still remember. A time when the world was considered a big place and far-away countries were hardly spoken of let alone known about.

"As I promised, I, Mon-Ka, Emperor of Mars..." the voice crackled with intermittent static like it was coming from a distant place, *"am once again making contact with your planet in the hope of initiating communications with you and your leaders."*

At the town limit, a sign shuddered as a dust devil whipped past in a sudden updraft, spinning a miniature dust tornado powerful enough that sometimes it could throw you off your bike. Shadows of moving oak branches splashed street light onto the weathered hand-painted sign that read Welcome to Empire - Gateway to the Swan Valley. Some townies wanted a new sign but nobody remembered who had painted this one so it was rarely discussed at town meetings anymore.

"People of Earth, I must once again tell you that your leaders have been keeping my existence from you," the voice crackled again.

On the deserted main street, the Crescent Cafe was open. Sam Wong, the owner, looked out through the window as the same dust devil whipped up some dirt that settled almost as soon as it spun around. Sam shrugged and returned back to his well-worn chair behind the counter and waited for customers. It was a slow night. Most nights were slow. Saturday night was when all the stores were open and parents shopped and farm kids and towners would chase each other along the side streets.

"They have chosen to suppress this information, but we believe you should know about us. I have so much to tell you about the universe, so much for you to marvel at," the voice said with firmness this time. Sam heard it over his radio but didn't

really pay much attention. And his English wasn't that good to begin with.

But a few blocks away from Main street past the lumberyard and past the hardware store and tucked into the back lot of a big white house stood an odd-looking home. Actually it was a garage or at least at one time it was. Now it had the big wide door sealed and painted over and a regular door had been cut and framed so as to make it look like a real house. But it was still a garage. And it was where Matthew lived with his mother and his grandmother.

A movie poster from The Day The Earth Stood Still featured prominently on the wall of Matthew's tiny bedroom. The garage had been fashioned into four rooms, a kitchen, a living room and two bedrooms. While it wasn't anything of the nature of some of the bedrooms Matthew had seen in other kid's homes, it still was his own room and the decor reflected that very much.

There were cut-out movie magazine pictures pinned on the walls, pictures of cowboy heroes like Roy Rogers and actors like Doris Day and James Dean. A small bed was pushed against the wall and an even smaller worn desk tucked against it that someone had given his mother. The other wall had a narrow old wood dresser pushed against it, another gift from someone that had no use for it anymore. All in all, this may have been the smallest bedroom in the whole world, but it was Matthew's bedroom. And his world.

The voice spoke again, *"But you must not believe your leaders. I, the Emperor of Mars, will tell you the secrets of our universe exactly one week of your time from today. I will arrive on Earth at Eleven P.M, October 31st, and I will speak over your radio waves."*

With that, the broadcast ended for a few seconds as Matthew turned the frequency dial on his plastic radio so that he could find the distant station again. He was a sturdy twelve-year old with dark hair and a full face that seemed to smile even when he didn't want it to. Matthew was pretty much normal or at least as normal as a guy could be living in a house that was really a garage. He was the kind of boy who had the gift of curiosity, he was interested in almost everything, from how his radio worked to why there were clouds or what made some people funny and others not.

His curiosity sometimes annoyed his mother who didn't always have answers. She had never made it past the eighth grade when her father took her out of school after her mother died and she had to do all the housework and chores. But that was when work was harder on the farms near town, now they had tractors and lots of equipment that made it easier for fewer people to work the farms. Matthew finally found the radio station frequency as an announcer's voice came across the air waves."

"And that was the message left by Mon Ka, who calls himself the Emperor of Mars. Both government and military officials dismiss the recording as a hoax," the announcer said in strong confident tones.

Matthew looked up at Michael Rennie, the actor whose solemn face looked down on him from the movie poster. Rennie was an imposing figure standing in front of a flying saucer, with his giant robot bodyguard Gort behind him. Matthew's eyes turned to Gort, looking at him.

"However, several UFO sightings have been reported over the skies of Los Angeles as over other parts of the western U.S. and Canada," the announcer's voice continued. Matthew listened to every word, almost holding his breath.

This was world-shocking news or at least it was to him. He lived in a small town where nothing really ever happened, where he knew almost every living person and every dog and cat as well. He wondered where everyone was at this very minute, were they also at their radios?

"Whether Mon-Ka is real or a hoax remains a mystery at this time. Locally, police have reported nothing unusual and anticipate the usual flying saucer sightings that often accompany these stories," the announcer added. The static became heavier and the signal disappeared from the radio.

That was the first time Matthew heard about the Emperor of Mars. Being twelve, he didn't know what to think, part of him was scared but another part seemed to want to know more about this voice who said he was the Emperor of Mars.

Instead he looked down at his scribbler, where he'd written the date - October 31. Then he turned towards his desk, where a photograph sat by a plastic flying saucer. The photo featured a smiling young man in his early 20's. It was Matthew's father, a father he never knew, it was a memory Matthew only imagined. His father was killed in the world war and that was the only certain thing Matthew knew about the man who now smiled at him from the picture frame.

He always wondered what it was like to have a father, almost all the kids in town had fathers and they seemed to complain about it a whole lot more than not. This seemed odd to Matthew, he felt that he was missing something not having a dad but he wasn't really sure what it was that he missed. Someone once told him "you can't miss what you never had," and maybe that was as good an answer as Matthew could ever find. Still he wondered about it. But right now, he was more concerned about the message he'd just heard on the radio.

That was real.

2

But as Matthew dealt with the Emperor of Mars, something else was about to happen. Not far away across town and in the shadow of the tall grain elevators sat a small house. It was a ramshackle combination of an original shed with a room that had been added on to form a makeshift house. The house was known by the children in town as "Nicodemus's Place," a place that was generally regarded as a haunted house, or at the very least, an odd one. Nobody ever explained why but the place had built up a collection of stories inspired more by gossip than reality. As far as anyone knew, no monsters or ghosts ever came from the shack.

Beyond the shack was a wheat field, and being fall, the wheat was waist-high to a man, and almost head-high to a twelve-year old. Wheat was what was grown in this part of the country; it was brought to the grain elevators and stored in huge storage bins that could hold thousands of bushels of wheat. Then, a train would arrive with boxcars attached, and each boxcar would be pulled under the long tube that swung into place over the boxcar. The wheat would be funneled down into the boxcar until it was filled. Sometimes there was so much wheat that it could take two whole days to fill an entire train. After that the train left with its cargo of wheat that sometimes would stretch for nearly a mile.

Since Matthew had never really traveled further than a few miles from town, he could only go by what he'd heard. The wheat traveled hundreds of miles, maybe thousands, all the way across the country. It would be taken to mills where it was ground into flour for bread and into cereals and a thousand other things. Matthew had seen pictures in school books about these far-away places, sometimes the wheat even went into huge ships that carried the cargo across the oceans. But oceans were a million miles away to Matthew. Still, one day he hoped to see them, to follow the route that the wheat took. But that wouldn't be soon.

Suddenly, a bolt of lightning flashed across the field near Nicodemus's place. Magnetic sounds clattered in the darkness and ball lightning zapped streaks around the elevator in brilliant blues and greens.

A dog on Nicodemus's porch sat up and growled. Several other dogs from town awoke and joined in the chorus. A crack of thunder erupted in the black sky.

Nicodemus Johnson opened his door, the warm orange light bled out into the darkness. Slowly, Nicodemus stepped out. It was hard to figure his age, he'd be called a young man by older people, and while he had a familiar look about him, like someone you knew, there was a distance to him. You'd notice him on the street, but wouldn't really know why.

"What is it, Dog?"

The dog wasn't about to let up. A flash of light from the field persuaded Nicodemus to walk towards it. As he walked, a soft rain began to patter to the ground. Nicodemus could smell the soft thudding of rain drops on the ground. It was one of those earthy scents that only people who live close to the land can smell. When Nicodemus reached the edge of the field he stopped.

A soft glow surrounded the field. Greenish-blue, it danced around madly with sparkles of static electricity discharging in all directions. Nicodemus could feel the magnetism in the air as the hairs on his arms stiffened. He had seen the Northern Lights before, Aurora Borealis, as he had learned was their real name. But they were high in the night sky and they only came out now and then. And they never were seen so low to the ground. And to the best of his memory, they never danced around tall stalks of wheat. And even as he watched, the sparkles and lights connected to his hand and danced up onto his shoulders. Who are you?" Nicodemus shouted to the darkness.

Nothing answered back as the sparkles and lights suddenly shot upwards into the night sky. Now Nicodemus stood there alone, rain pelting down harder now, drenching him. He didn't move, rather he just stood there listening and watching. It was like he was waiting for something. Or someone.

At the same time, across town and in his bedroom, Matthew listened to the rain pelting down on his roof. It was always a comforting sound, being that he was snug and cozy under his blanket. Except, this time, there was something different about it. And Matthew had an odd thought, something that came from that place within him that fears and uncertainty came from. Matthew wondered if the world would still be there tomorrow.

3

The town was still there in the morning as sunlight brought a new day's warmth to Empire. Matthew's mother, Elana, poured milk into a bowl of oatmeal that sat lifelessly in front of Matthew. He studied it reluctantly, his favorite was bacon and eggs, but that was only for Sundays. He knew from school that some of the kids in town had it on other days as well. But for Matthew, it was a rare treat. On school days he got oatmeal.

"Eat, you have school."

"No more rice krispies?"

"Oatmeal."

"I hate oatmeal."

Elana walked back to the stove, "Your father said food should always be eaten. We are lucky to have food when people in the old country have little."

The old country. Whenever she couldn't think of an answer that would convince him otherwise she would always say "the old country". Matthew never knew the old country, except that it sounded like a horrible place where people lived even more poorly than Matthew did. He had seen photographs of people in thick, bad-fitting clothes and who rarely smiled. His only connection to that sad old country was his grandmother Babka.

Babka knelt in the living room, mumbling prayers to herself. This usually took a half hour and Matthew never really understood why it took her so long. She was in her 70's and knew little English. Babka was always dressed in black; in fact, Matthew didn't think she had anything else. There was a multi-colored dress that she sometimes wore but for most of her days she dressed in black. She was his father's mother and the three of them were the only family they had. "Why does Babka pray so much?

"She prays for your father, and many others. It wouldn't hurt you either."

"I don't know as many dead people as she does."

"You will," she answered with as much as a look, "Eat, I have to go to clean Dr. Collins house this morning. And go straight to school. And stay away from the elevators."

Matthew had his head in a comic book.

"Did you hear me?"

Matthew dug his spoon into the bowl. "Yes, I heard you." He ate fast as he had a mission before school and there was just enough time.

4

At the bottom of the 10-story grain elevator was the place where trucks dumped their grain. The massive grain storage bin had a grid of metal bars over it. The bars were strong enough for big trucks to drive onto it and tilt their truckbeds on an angle that allowed the hundreds of bushels of wheat to fall down between the bars. Then it was weighed and then sent up long shafts to the storage areas of the elevator. It was also a place where kids were not allowed.

Matthew stepped onto the twenty foot long scale. The space between the bars was about two inches, certainly not enough to fall through, unless you were a ladybug or maybe a mouse but more than enough to hold him. After all trucks weighing thousands of pounds could stand here too. Yet, with his movement, the entire grid moved just enough to feel the sensation.

"No way," a voice behind him echoed.

Matthew turned to the voice. Bernie Bernstein stood on solid ground, not about to move to where Matthew stood. Bernie was twelve too and a little bit heavier than Matthew. Some kids teased Bernie about his weight but he wasn't one to take it very much. Bernie had his share of fights so now most of the kids who enjoyed teasing other kids left him alone.

Matthew moved his body a little. The grid moved slightly.

"Come on." Matthew challenged.

"We gotta go to school."

"Chicken."

"We're not supposed to be here."

As if to tempt Bernie more, Matthew walked further onto the grid. Bernie took a few steps forward. He reached the edge of the grid, closed his eyes and stepped onto it. It moved slightly. He stepped back.

"You can do it, scaredy-cat."

"I don't want to do it."

Matthew stared at him then shook his head. Bernie finally relented. He stepped on the grid again.

Then he took another step. The grid shifted slightly. At the same time, a voice bellowed from the darkness above them.

"What are you kids doing?"

Bernie jumped back and ran for the outside. Matthew turned to see Nicodemus's silhouette climbing down. The grid shifted with his added weight and Matthew turned and ran outside. Nicodemus watched them run away.

"Darn kids, you can hurt yourself in here!"

The words were lost as Matthew and Bernie had already disappeared.

The main street was beginning to show signs of life. Some of the thirty or so businesses were opening. Sam Wong's was always the first to open and the last to close. He stared out the window with the same passive look as he had the night before hardly noticing Matthew and Bernie walk past.

"There's a new cowboy movie showing tonight," Matthew said. Bernie shrugged, "Naw, I don't wanna see a cowboy movie. Besides, we're getting a television."

Matthew's attention suddenly became sharper.

"You are? When?"

"Soon, my dad's gonna put it in the lobby so hotel guests can watch."

Matthew held back his excitement, "What about us?"

"We can watch it too," Bernie answered, "But I gotta be in bed by nine."

The Jenkins house stood on a lot a half block off Main Street. Mrs. Jenkins owned the two-story house by herself since her husband had passed away a few years ago.

Being a sociable woman who enjoyed card games and visitors she had decided to take in a boarder who could provide some company especially during the long winters when it was harder to get out. Mrs. Jenkins preferred professional people but in a farm community there were few professional people who didn't have their own home. That was why she was delighted when a certain Miss Major asked to be considered. Miss Major was the new school teacher for Grade Six.

Miss Major was the hit of the town from the day she arrived. She was barely twenty having gone to school somewhere far enough away from Empire that nobody knew her family or her friends. She had gone to Teacher's College for the obligatory one-year program and had graduated with her teacher's certificate. And then for some reason she picked Empire.

Miss Major was the stuff of boyhood dreams, young, pretty with shining hair down to her shoulders and a smile that melted a young boy's heart and most likely older boys too. As she stepped outside she saw Mrs. Jenkins was already trimming flowers along the white picket fence.

"Good morning, Mrs. Jenkins," Miss Major smiled.

"Good morning to you, Miss Major," Mrs. Jenkins replied, "a lovely day."

"Yes," Miss Major answered back, "I'll see you later."

Miss Major opened the gate and walked out onto the sidewalk, carrying a leather briefcase filled with school assignments and other things unknown to twelve-year old boys and girls. Her hair bounced in the sunlight as she walked with athletic strides down towards Main Street. Then she arrived at the corner, turned to her right and walked into someone approaching from the other side. Her briefcase fell to the sidewalk, opening up and scattering some of her papers. Miss Major recovered, suddenly realizing she was looking right at Nicodemus who already had knelt to pick up the papers.

"Oh, I am so sorry, I wasn't..." she started to say.

Nicodemus stood up and handed her the papers. "My fault," he mumbled. And with that, he walked past her. Miss Major watched him go.

"Um, thank you..." she said even though he had already gone far enough that he didn't hear her. He climbed into his old truck and drove off without as much as a look. And he didn't notice Matthew and Bernie as his truck passed them and turned a corner. "Nicodemus is sure weird sometimes," Bernie said. "He was in the war like my dad," Matthew said. "Didya know he used to live on Thunder Hill?"

Matthew nodded, "So what?"

"You know what everyone says about Thunder Hill." Bernie answered.

Matthew knew all the stories, it was one of the first things you learned as a kid here. "That it came up in the night all of a sudden," Matthew answered.

"Yeah, it's an Indian spiritual place," Bernie continued. "An' there's ghosts there too."

"There's no ghosts on Thunderhill and Nicodemus isn't a ghost," Matthew said, "He just looks after the elevators."

A radio played from a nearby house reminding Matthew of the news he wanted to tell Bernie.

"There's an Emperor of Mars coming to earth, did you know?"

Bernie turned to his friend, "that's dopey."

"I heard it on the radio."

"Yeah, then why didn't my mom and dad tell me?"

"Maybe they don't know."

"Yeah, sure. You're just makin' it up, like you always do."

Matthew's eyes narrowed, it always came to this with Bernie when he didn't believe Matthew. "Am not," Matthew countered. "Like when you said Roy Rogers was going to come here. Or when you said Doris Day wrote to you. That was just a dopey picture someone in her office sent you. She never even signed it, I bet."

Matthew moved ahead of Bernie a few steps to show his anger, "she did sign it."

As the two boys walked towards the three-story brick school at the end of the street, something else was happening across town at the elevators.

Tom Anderson hit his horn as he waited to enter onto the giant scale with a full four tons of wheat in his truck. There was no sign of Nicodemus. That was when he looked toward the same field that Nicodemus had looked at last night. Anderson noticed something odd. Something he couldn't quite believe. Just then Nicodemus arrived in his truck and saw Anderson staring at the field in disbelief. Whatever he was looking at was something he had never seen before.

Something Nicodemus had already seen.

5

The school was typical of small towns across the Midwest. It was built of bricks in 1915 to handle the first wave of new immigrants to this part of the country. They came mostly from Eastern Europe fleeing the cruelty of the Russian Czar who took most of their crops as payment for taxes, leaving them with barely enough to survive the harsh winters.

It always started the same, a brother or an uncle would immigrate here then he would write home to tell how land was practically given away. The country needed settlers and these people had nothing to lose and everything to gain. They gathered their few belongings and found enough money to take ships from Europe to North America landing in New York or Montreal and then headed to meet their relatives who had already settled and bought land.

There were others too, Swedes and Germans and many others. And mostly they got along as working dawn to dark left little time to find differences among the tribes.

The immigrants had large families as they had more children they had the more workers for their farms. Everyone pitched in to raise crops that they would sell and for the first time would be able to keep the money.

It didn't take long for the schools to appear and this one in Empire was typical of its era. It was three stories high and usually it was the biggest building in the small towns that dotted the prairies. Towns were built along the railroad lines every eight miles. Eight miles meant that if a train broke down the furthest anyone would have to walk was four miles for help.

The school had grades one through twelve although sometimes two grades were to be found in the same room. There were about one hundred students from the town itself and then maybe another hundred from the farms too close to town to have their own school.

Matthew ran past the gate and into the schoolyard, passing a few farm kids who were usually early for school as they had farm chores that began before the sun came up. They looked different than the townies, their clothes were more like work clothes than school clothes and they wore thick laced boots that usually carried the smell of the animals that most farmers had. Matthew was poor but at least he had school clothes, even if most were hand-me-downs from people Elana knew or worked for.

But right now, something was on his mind and nothing could get in the way. He crashed through the doors and ran two flights of stairs. Outside Bernie was breathing hard and chose to walk instead. Besides he knew why Matthew was in such a hurry.

Matthew burst into the classroom and immediately crashed into a desk. He caught himself in time, just before Miss Major turned around from the blackboard.

"Matthew, are you all right?"

Matthew straightened the desk and tried to ignore the pain in his knee. "I... I'm sorry I'm late, Miss Major," he answered. She smiled softly, a smile to melt the biggest iceberg. "It's all right," she said, "just as long as you didn't hurt yourself." The words spun Matthew like those fluffy cottonwood balls that drifted with the wind on a fall day. He was in heaven. Or at least, that place where the world is a wonderful thing. Especially when the most beautiful girl in the world asked if he was all right. He remembered why he was here and quickly headed to the blackboards where he began to put chalk into the railing that held them along with erasers. This was his job every morning, to prepare the classroom. At first Miss Major said he didn't have to do it but he insisted until she gave in. It was his only time alone with her, when he could watch while she prepared her assignments.

"It's a beautiful morning, don't you think?"

Matthew pretended to be sorting the chalks, some of which were shorter than the others. He nodded, "Yeah." He glanced at the clock, nearly nine o'clock. Some of the students entered and Matthew realized his morning time with Miss Major was again coming to an end.

Back by the elevators, Anderson was still staring off at the field. Finally he turned to Nicodemus who was waiting for him to drive his truck onto the scale.

"What happened there?" Anderson asked.

Nicodemus didn't bother to look as he set the scale controls for Anderson's truck.

"Don't know."

"Did you see it?" Anderson asked again.

Nicodemus stopped working for a second and looked back at the field. He thought for a moment deciding on what words would best suit Anderson's questions.

"Yeah, I saw it," he answered.

Then Nicodemus stepped back and waited for Anderson to drive the truck onto the scale. Anderson glanced back at the field again, shook his head and mumbled something. He climbed into his truck and drove it onto the scale.

Nicodemus turned to look back at the field for a moment. Yes, he thought, he had seen it early this morning and he still wasn't quite sure what it meant. But whatever it was out there on the field it brought an ominous feeling to him.

A feeling that things in Empire were going to change.

6

The class sat quietly as Gloria Taylor spoke. Gloria was twelve going on thirty, straight A's, and she shopped for her clothes in the city. Matthew had never been to the city, in fact, most of the kids had never been there either.

"And so it is widely believed by political experts that, with the United States and the Soviet Union both voting against the invasion of Egypt by British, French and Israeli forces, the conflict will come to an end very soon," Gloria said with an authoritative composure.

Matthew and Bernie exchanged bored looks. Two desks away, Stephanie Simpson tried to get Matthew's attention but couldn't quite get it. Stephanie was pretty, smart and nice to most everyone, she was friendly and helpful and someone you could always trust. But right now she was frustrated as Matthew wasn't noticing her hand waving just enough so Miss Major wouldn't see. Finally Stephanie handed a note to the girl between her and Matthew. The girl took a second to read the message, giggled to herself and then smugly passed it over to Matthew.

One of the other girls, Nancy Carsen, caught Bernie's eye for a second and smiled at him. Bernie awkwardly turned away, then back. Yes, she was smiling at him. He smiled back.

Meanwhile, Gloria continued to read, oblivious of the class's lack of attention.

"But, Egypt has called for all Moslem countries to fight the allied forces as a sacred duty and it is possible that the Soviets will intercede on behalf of the Egyptians. If this occurs, the Suez conflict could develop into a major war, much like Korea."

Matthew opened the note, it read "See you after school?" There was a big heart drawn around the words. He looked at Stephanie who gazed lovingly into his eyes. He rolled his eyes and turned away.

"That was a very good report on the Suez conflict, Gloria," Miss Major said. "You've spent some time researching it. Very good."

Gloria beamed," Thank you, Miss Major. There's much more to discuss on the subject, I thought that my fellow classmates could offer their views," she smiled.

There was a collective horrified gasp among her "fellow classmates" and Miss Major caught the heads looking anywhere but at Gloria or Miss Major. Anything would be better than discussing topics with Gloria. As the discussion was a little too complex for a Grade 6 class, Miss Major favored giving the others a break this time

"That's a very good idea, Gloria, but perhaps next time," Miss Major said.

Gloria's smile faded a little, but she graciously conceded. All eyes now turned away, hoping to avoid being called.

"Paul," Miss Major called. Paul looked up, he was a bleary-eyed twelve year old in the corner who looked like he just woke up. He always looked like he just woke up. It took him a second to realize Miss Major was talking to him.

"Uh, I don't know, Miss Major, I forgot this is current event day," he answered.

"It seems you forgot last week also," Miss Major said. Paul smiled in that awkward way which he hoped would free him from attention, "I guess I forget a lot."

The others giggled as Matthew opened his scribbler to a page with only the heading Current Events written in pencil. There was nothing else on the page. Fear began to creep into his mind as Miss Major scanned the class, searching for a new victim. She stopped at

Stephanie who smiled, ready as always to participate in class. Miss Major had a quick thought, girls are always ready and she decided she'd put more pressure on the boys.

Miss Major's eyes fell on Bernie who shifted nervously. She passed him and turned her look towards Matthew. Matthew could feel the intensity. It would be him. It was a funny thing how everyone else in the room now knew that they were saved. That a victim had been found for the sacrifice. Matthew closed his eyes and tried to will away the class, even Miss Major. Maybe when he opened his eyes, they would all be gone.

"Matthew," the word echoed to Matthew, like a distant thunderstorm.

Matthew glanced over at Bernie who flashed a "you're on your own" look. Matthew slowly turned to look at her.

"Miss Major?"

"Matthew, you may give us your current event."

Matthew rose slowly as the class waited with eagerness to watch Matthew face certain death. Like the lions awaited the Christians.

Slowly, the class disappeared in his mind, he was spinning in a world of his own, sounds echoed, a car outside the window, the scratching of a pencil on a scribbler near him, Miss Major waiting for him to speak. Matthew took a deep breath.

"As my current event, I am going to report on…"

Silence. Matthew froze. His life would be nothing if he lost Miss Major's favor. The mornings helping her with the classroom would be over, the future would be gone. The world would end. Matthew looked down at the empty page and then noticed something scribbled at the bottom - October 31. Suddenly he had an idea.

"That…" he started.

Bernie rolled his eyes as a few giggles bubbled up from the class. Gloria waited with a cruel smile.

"That the Emperor of Mars is coming to Earth next week."

The students glanced around at each other, some daring to look at Miss Major for her reaction. Stephanie smiled as she looked at Matthew with a smile. Then the silence was broken as Miss Major stood up, "The Emperor of Mars?" she asked.

Matthew had been given a period of grace. Now he had to follow up. "Yes Miss Major, the Emperor of Mars is coming to Earth on…" he stammered, "on October 31st and he's going to tell all the secrets of the universe to us."

This time the class laughed. Stephanie didn't, she wouldn't dream of hurting Matthew's feeling. Not the boy she adored. Never.

Bernie was still Matthew's best friend but even he thought that Matthew had pushed the envelope this time. Bernie just shook his head in silence while his friend was making a fool out of himself. And that might pass over to him as well.

Miss Major felt for Matthew, and she worked to get up an appropriate look with some seriousness. "That'll be enough, class," she said quietly. Then she looked at Matthew, "I'm not familiar with that story, Matthew."

"I heard it on the radio," Matthew suddenly answered, "People have been seeing flying saucers everywhere."

Miss Major felt his desperation and decided to change direction. "I think your assignment should be a little more down to earth," she said.

"But it was on the radio," Matthew pleaded.

Matthew looked for help around the class. Bernie lowered his head. Only Stephanie looked at him, nodding her sympathy. Matthew closed his eyes again, wishing for this moment to be gone forever.

7

"Boy, I don't believe you said that Emperor of Mars stuff," Bernie said as both boys walked home after school. "It's true," Matthew answered, "He's gonna tell us the secrets of the universe."

"Would you trust a Martian?" Bernie asked, "I mean if there were Martians, they'd probably wanna vaporize us."

"He's different."

Bernie stopped and looked straight at Matthew, "no Martians are gonna come to Earth."

Bernie said sharply, "Kids think you belong in the nut house already, remember that time you said there was a cowboy fort at the river, and we spent a whole day looking for guns and arrowheads.

Then Miss Major said there were never any forts around here. Now Martians?"

Matthew looked at Bernie, "It's true, Bernie, it was on the radio." Bernie rolled his eyes in the manner he had watched his dad roll his eyes when he didn't quite believe something.

"Hi Matthew," a girl's voice said behind him. It was Stephanie. Stephanie approached the two boys as they kept walking. She walked faster to keep even with them.

"I gotta go home," Bernie said and turned and ran off, leaving Matthew with Stephanie. Matthew looked straight ahead, trying to avoid any eye contact.

"Wanna come to my house?" Stephanie asked.

"I can't."

"Why not?"

"'Cause I can't."

"Then where are you going?"

Matthew continued walking as he turned on Main Street. Stephanie moved faster to keep up. "I know. You're going to my dad's store to watch the TV, that's where all the men go and sit around and talk. Why can't I go with you?"

"You're just a kid, that's why," Matthew answered.

"Matthew I'm eleven and you're twelve." Stephanie countered.

"That's what I mean, I'm older." Matthew said. And with that he ran off leaving Stephanie alone. She shouted, "Possession is nine-tenths of the law. And that TV is mine too." But her words faded away on the nearly empty street. Stephanie stood alone for the longest time, her temper soothing a little. She had known Matthew since they were in the first grade and had fell for him right from the start. She remembered the second grade when she and Matthew had worked together on an art project and he actually talked to her for most of the year. But Grade Three changed him, as he began to play baseball and hung around with the other boys. By Grade Five, he seemed to be mostly by himself, except for Bernie.

Her life was different than his, she lived with her father and mother and brother Tommy in a big house where everyone had their own room. They had a lawn and a driveway, something that Matthew didn't have as she had passed his house often hoping that he would be outside and that he would see her. He never did but she had the gift of patience and the satisfaction of persistence and Stephanie knew it would all work out just fine.

Then something odd happened. For just a second, Stephanie noticed a bright light in the sky, brighter than the sun. But just as fast as it sparked, it was gone. Stephanie's look fell from the sky to the grain elevators, which seemed to be just below the bright light. Something seemed to chill her, a feeling that she was being watched, a feeling that something was up there in the big open sky.

Stephanie ran down the street as fast as she could.

8

Stephanie ran all the way to her father's hardware and surplus store, not stopping until she was inside. She spotted Matthew sitting beside the black and white television set that her father kept to entertain the locals not to mention possibly increase his business.

Simpson's store was a combination of hardware merchandise like hammers and shovels and nails. But it also carried army surplus things like ammunition boxes from the war that could be recycled to hold nails or tools or almost anything. There were military coats, military shoes, rain gear, army helmets, camping gear and even some silk parachutes and one big aerial weather balloon that Simpson would inflate once a year for the annual harvest parade.

The store was also a hangout for local farmers and businessmen, a place where they could come for a soda or coffee and spend an hour or two catching up with the local gossip.

And today was no different as a handful of men sat around "chewing the fat," as Stephanie's mother described it.

Matthew sat in front of the television set watching the afternoon movie. Usually it was a western and Stephanie knew that those were Matthew's favorites. The picture was a little fuzzy since the antenna on top of the set wasn't able to receive a good signal. The television station was about eighty miles away so unless you had an antenna mounted on the roof you'd get a fuzzy picture. Still, it was better than nothing.

Stephanie pulled a chair beside Matthew and sat down beside him. Matthew had noticed her almost immediately but tried to focus on the movie he was watching. Stephanie didn't push her luck and instead sat quietly watching the movie.

Stephanie's father, Simpson, sat holding court with three other men, some of whom drank cool sodas. He was a tall, overbearing man in his 40's, who liked to lead the discussions.

After all, it was his store. And Simpson was also the town policeman not that it was a big deal. Simpson still liked to wear the badge even though he never wore the old uniform that had been passed to him by the former policeman when he retired.

Matthew was very careful around Simpson as he didn't care much for Eastern European people like Matthew and his mother and wasn't afraid to tell them so. He had been like that since he went to the same war that Matthew's father had gone to. But unlike his father, Simpson came back alive. It was best to be seen and not heard as far as Matthew figured, and as long as he sat quietly watching the movie and not drawing attention to himself, things would be all right. Simpson glanced at Stephanie and Matthew for a second and then turned to the others, one of whom was Anderson.

"So Anderson here says something landed on Nicodemus' field." Simpson said. All eyes trained on Anderson who fidgeted, realizing that his credibility was on the line here. The last thing he wanted was to be considered odd or misinformed.

"Saw what I saw," Anderson answered with a quiet nod.

Lorne Everett perked up. Lorne was eighteen, fresh out of school, wearing blue jeans and a leather jacket and had recently grown sideburns on his face, considered something of a rebellious signature in town.

This and the Harley Davidson motorcycle that Lorne had salvaged from a wrecking yard made him a prime candidate for the town Marlon Brando impersonator. Brando was the movie star who starred in a movie about motorcycle gangs that Matthew had seen a year ago.

"Didn't you hear about that Martian who's supposed to come to Earth? There's been a whole pile of flying saucer sightings," Lorne said.

Matthew glanced over at the men, now listening to every word. Stephanie caught his look and turned her attention to the men as well. Simpson shook his head, "Only unidentified flying object round Empire is that Harley Davidson you run around on. And if you don't get a haircut soon folks are gonna think you're from outer space."

The other men chuckled over this, waiting for the next jab.

"Any Martians come around here and you'd probably skedaddle into that bomb shelter of yours." Lorne responded. But this time the mood turned quiet. Lorne had crossed an invisible line by addressing a sensitive subject that was known but not talked about. At least openly.

"It's a root cellar, Lorne," Simpson said with a finality that meant the subject was closed. A lot of people in town had root cellars beneath their houses. That was where they stored onions and potatoes from their gardens as well as other storable vegetables. This was common in a small town where most people had gardens for their vegetables rather than buying them at a store. Bomb shelters were another story and one few liked to bring up.

After the war, the world settled down to a time of peace, at least until America and Russia began building atomic bombs in a race that became known as the Cold War. It was not really a war by the usual standards as the two countries never really fought each other but rather they built up their military strengths in the hopes that neither would attack. But many people worried that if there ever was a war the power of a thousand atomic bombs would leave little of the Earth to live on.

So bomb shelters became a fashion of sorts, they would be built underground so that if an atomic war happened a family could escape to their underground shelter. It would be equipped with food and lamps and batteries and all sorts of things that would allow them to survive for up to a year without coming out.

It was well known that Simpson had built such a bomb shelter but that he never admitted to it. Some thought it was because if a bomb fell, Simpson didn't necessarily want to share his bomb shelter with anyone else. His bomb shelter was probably one of two or three known to have been built in town.

"Root cellars don't need three foot concrete walls. Wally Dan says you asked him about his shelter. Either for Russians or spacemen, way I see it," Lorne answered back. "You oughtta not go talking about what you don't know anything about, kid," Simpson answered.

The mood changed quickly, the other men remained silent as nobody wanted to speak up now especially when Simpson was in a bad mood. This did not fare well for Matthew who now came into Simpson's view.

"Stephanie, you'd best get home." Simpson barked. Stephanie looked over at Matthew who kept his eyes on the television set. Sometimes Simpson's grumpiness would go away if left alone and not challenged. Stephanie tried to get Matthew's look but he wasn't going to take a chance of losing his seat in front of the TV. "Stephanie, get home," Simpson repeated.

Stephanie finally gave up. She slipped off the chair and looked at Matthew. But he wasn't offering any comfort. It was bad enough that she followed him here to this special place where men sat around and talked but she was also drawing attention to his very presence. This was something that Matthew tried to avoid knowing Simpson's temper. Now anything could happen.

"I guess I have to go now, Matthew," she said, hoping for an answer. But Matthew kept his eyes on the snowy picture on the television set. "Bye," she finally said, with a curl of her lip that indicated very well that she was not pleased. She spun around and walked out of the store. Matthew turned to watch her go avoiding any eye contact with Simpson Finally, it came.

"Don't you have something else to do but sit an' watch my TV?" It costs money for electricity," Simpson said. Matthew pretended not to hear, maybe Simpson wouldn't notice. Lorne leaned forward, "Ain't gonna make you go broke, couple of kids watchin' TV," he said. But Simpson was already in a bad mood.

"You go home, boy," he said loudly.

Matthew shrugged as there was no way out now. He could come back again but the key to his being able to stay and watch television while the men talked was to become invisible. This meant no talking, no fidgeting and no trouble. Reluctantly, Matthew stood up and shuffled to the door past Lorne and the others. Lorne gave him a wink indicating that at least he was on Matthew's side. Simpson wasn't finished and as Matthew walked by, Simpson shook his head.

"Sometimes I wonder what the hell I was fighting for in the war," he said gruffly, "Come home and there's more foreigners here than over there." Lorne looked at Simpson, "You sure get miserable, you know that?" he said quietly.

9

Outside, back on Main Street, Matthew trudged along. He was used to Simpson's comments about people from other countries that came here to live and he didn't really understand what was different about him and his mother and grandmother that made Simpson so mean.

There were others in town who whispered behind his mother's back. Matthew had noticed this when they were at the food market. It was mostly the business people or the rich people who had big houses and big farms.

To be truthful Matthew didn't like some of their kids, they were the ones like Gloria who wore new clothes almost every day and who had the best toys and the biggest birthday parties.

"Hey Hunky," a voice shouted.

Matthew froze, the day was getting worse and it wasn't even close to ending. That voice was not what he wanted to hear right now.

Slowly he turned around to face the voice's owner.

Tommy Simpson was a chip off the old block, as the adults would say. He was a young kid version of his dad but mostly he was a bully to every younger kid in town. At fourteen, Tommy had terrorized every boy from Grade One to Grade Six. And he seemed to especially not like Matthew from the very first time they set eyes on each other, when Matthew was in Grade 2. The odd thing about the Simpson's was that Stephanie was so different. In fact, one time when Tommy was pushing Matthew and Bernie around, Stephanie came to their rescue and telling Tommy to go away. Which he eventually did.

The only trouble with that was that everyone knew within hours that a girl had saved Matthew and Bernie. A thing like that could hang around a kid's neck for years and years, maybe forever.

Matthew looked for an escape. Tommy was standing right in front of him but there was space to the left. Matthew made a move to the left but Tommy blocked him off and grabbed him by his shirt.

"Where's that money you owe me, hunky?" Tommy said.

Hunky was a mean term for Matthew's Eastern European ethnicity. Matthew didn't know where it came from and nobody ever could tell him what it meant even his mother. But secretly he thought that she really did know but that it was too cruel to tell Matthew. Whatever it meant, it wasn't nice. And Matthew had only one choice.

"I... I don't owe you anything," he stammered.

"I don't owe you anything," Tommy mimicked in a high-pitched mocking voice, "Is that right? Well, I say you owe me twenty-five cents each week. For protection."

Matthew swallowed hard, somehow this time he was not going to give in to Tommy. He wasn't even sure why he felt that way but something inside of him said he had to make a stand. Just like the people in the movies did. But he had to also be ready for the consequences and he started to imagine what a punch in the face would feel like. Then he gathered his courage.

"I don't have any money, Tommy," he said quietly.

Tommy grabbed Matthew's hand and pulled his thumb backwards. "Guess I'm gonna have to persuade you," Tommy said. Matthew's eyes narrowed, waiting for the pain, ready to deal with it as it came.

"Where's your fatso friend now, huh," Tommy said, "See, you should never trust his kind, they stick together, just like you hunkies, my dad says." Suddenly Tommy stopped. His eyes looked up past Matthew, higher up. Someone was approaching, still unseen by Matthew. Then just as quickly Tommy let go of Matthew and ran off.

Matthew turned slowly to face a tall shadow standing in sunlight – the face was dark in shadow but the figure was familiar. It was Nicodemus.

"Did he hurt you?" Nicodemus asked in his usual gruff voice. Matthew felt a tear in his eye and quickly wiped it away hoping that Nicodemus hadn't seen it.

"No."

"That boy is trouble," Nicodemus said in a noticeably softer voice. Matthew wasn't sure what to say then finally came up with something. "Uh, thanks," he said to Nicodemus. Nicodemus started to walk away and another idea came suddenly to Matthew and he had to act quickly.

"Mr. Nicodemus..." Matthew said. Nicodemus turned around and looked back at

Matthew. This was what he wanted, to get Nicodemus's attention but now he had to follow up on it. Matthew whirled the words in his mind trying to choose the right ones.

"Speak up boy," Nicodemus answered. The words came out of Matthew's mouth faster than even he expected, and in a most direct way. "Did you see a flying saucer in your field today?" Matthew stared right at him.

Nicodemus looked back at the boy in silence. He also was trying to choose the words that would fit. It was the first time Matthew had seen Nicodemus stuck for words. His usual words were well known by Matthew, it was always "get out of here kids, stay away from here," or things like that. But now he seemed to have a hard time answering Matthew's question. Finally he answered.

"You boys keep away from the elevators, you could get hurt," was all Nicodemus said. He turned and Matthew watched him go. It was not the answer Matthew wanted and somehow Matthew felt, it was not the answer Nicodemus wanted either. He watched Nicodemus until he turned a corner and disappeared.

Then Matthew suddenly felt that someone was watching him, almost like Stephanie felt earlier. It didn't take long for his eyes to fall on the two grain elevators at the end of Main Street. He had seen them many times but this time there was something odd about the towers. Maybe it was the cloud floating in the blue sky that seemed to cover them in shadow. Maybe it was something else. Matthew turned and ran home as quickly as he could.

10

Even though it was a cemetery full of people who had died it always gave Matthew a safe feeling. The cemetery stood near the church that Matthew and his mother and grandmother attended every Sunday. The church was different than many of the other churches in the area. What made it different was the onion-shaped dome on the roof, a style that had been around since the ancient Byzantine empire of the mid-east. Matthew liked the fact that it was different. It gave him a special feeling about his ethnic background that even men like Simpson couldn't deny.

The cemetery had a slight slant due to a rolling hillside that offered a beautiful view of the open prairie. There were about sixty graves with headstones and about twenty crosses which Matthew had learned were older than the headstones. Some of the crosses were slowly disintegrating from the harsh winters and hot summers. Many of the headstones were written in Cyrillic alphabet, the language of most eastern-European people. Matthew never learned the written language but he liked the different shape of each letter as compared to English.

Right now he watched his mother clean weeds away from the grave where his father was buried. His father was one of the few whose body was returned, most of the soldiers who died in Europe were buried there. He glanced at the cameo photograph that was attached to the headstone which featured a photograph of Jacob, his father, youthful in a military uniform. This was the only contact that Matthew could remember since he was barely a year old when his father left for the war.

Elena knelt on the soft grass and pulled weeds from the grave with her hands, bunching them on a small pile that she would throw away later. Babka knelt by another cross and prayed silently, her mouth moving with each word. She glanced up at Matthew and caught him looking at his wristwatch.

The watch was a gift he didn't expect but it was probably one of his most precious things. It was an authentic copy of a Gene Autry watch, Autry being a famous cowboy movie star whose films Matthew had seen at the movie theater.

Elena had bought it for him last Christmas, an unexpected surprise as she rarely bought things they didn't need. She said it was so he knew when to come home and thus was practical. It was the only one of its kind in Empire and Matthew was extremely careful with it, never taking it out for playing or hiding it when Tommy came around. But right now it was telling him the time and he looked back towards the town, not far away.

"You have somewhere else to be?" Elana asked.

"The movie," he answered with some worry. The movie that was playing at the small theater a few blocks away.

"You always go to the movie. You don't have to go tonight."

"But it's a cowboy show."

"It costs money."

Money. That was the word that always stopped everything. Money was why Matthew couldn't always go to the movies, money was why he couldn't get new clothes like some of the other kids, money was why he ate oatmeal for breakfast rather than rice krispies. One day he would not have to worry about money.

"I've still got money from my birthday," Matthew pleaded.

"When I was your age I didn't have half the things you have now," Elana answered.

Matthew knew that he had to change the subject and get away from talking about money. It was his only chance to make the movie in time. His mind ran through possibilities. But there was only one really good distraction.

"Did you hear about the flying saucer that landed in Nicodemus's field?" Matthew said," Everybody was talking about it. Even Mr. Simpson." Elana just shook her head and finished pulling weeds. "Can't we visit your father without silly stories?" she said. She stood up and looked towards the setting sun. Matthew felt a little easier now. At least the movie discussion has been put on a back burner and he still had time to make it if they left soon. Elana walked over to Babka and helped her up. They were going home.

The movie theater had been a hall used for a church group that had long disbanded and only recently had been transformed into a movie theater. It had one hundred seats separated by a center aisle and was usually full on Fridays and Saturdays. There were two movies that played each week with, the first one playing from Monday to Wednesday, showing once a night at 8 pm. The second movie would run from

Thursday to Saturday with two shows on Saturday night. Very few of the movies were new, in fact some of them were quite old but they were still new as far as Matthew was concerned. He loved movies.

It all started when Matthew was around four when his mother had taken him to see his first movie. But his initial reaction had been less than happy, the images on the big screen, bigger than anything he had ever seen, only frightened him. Matthew broke out in tears crying loud enough for Elana to take him out. This might have been the end of Matthew's movie attending had not it been for the kindly projectionist, Mr. Kiminsky, who knew Elana and who offered to take Matthew for her while she watched the movie. Elana really hadn't wanted to but since she had paid for it, she thought it was the practical thing to do.

It was there in the projection room that Matthew first watched the film roll through the projector. It was like a fantasy with the octopus-like machine and its burning arc light that was brilliant enough to shine the image onto a screen nearly one hundred feet away.

While it looked scary, the projector ran with a soft clickety-clack rhythm that was very comforting, almost like being on a train. And the

warmth of the arc light made Matthew a little
sleepy as well. It was safer here near the
projector and as he grew up, the projectionist
sometimes let Matthew come upstairs and
watch the movie through the little window that
the projector's lens used to project the images. It
all seemed like magic to Matthew and he fell in
love with the movies.

But right now inside the theater, grotesque
spacemen were chasing a man and woman on
the big screen. It was a serial, a black and white
episode about 10 minutes long that featured
spacemen, monsters and jungle animals with a
hero and heroine always in danger. At the very
end they usually fell off a cliff or were in an
exploding spaceship. Then the serial ended with
a voiceover telling to audience to come back
next week for the next episode to see if the
heroes survived.

Matthew and Bernie ate boxes of popcorn, a
fairly expensive luxury at five cents a box, as
they watched the big screen, totally engrossed in
the action. Something caught Matthew's eye as
he watched the movie and he turned his
attention to a figure sitting a few rows on the
other side of the theater. It was Nicodemus. He
was watching the screen almost transfixed by
the images.

Matthew turned back to the action on the screen where the evil spacemen corner the hero and heroine in a cave, firing rayguns that rip the cave apart until the entire cave exploded. The screen action froze as a title appeared, DON'T MISS THE NEXT EPISODE OF - DEATH RAY FROM MARS!! COMING NEXT WEEK TO THIS THEATER. Matthew turned back to see Nicodemus but he was gone.

"They'll get out," Bernie said. Matthew turned back to Bernie. "Maybe not," he answered. "They always get out," Bernie repeated, looking around in the near darkness and noticing someone else. "There's your girlfriend," he continued. Matthew turned to where Bernie pointed. Seated in the row behind them were Stephanie and her mother Mrs. Simpson. Stephanie was looking not at the screen but at Matthew, having waited for a long time for him to turn around. She smiled and waved. Matthew turned back to the screen and slid down so low his head was barely visible.

Just then the screen lit up in brilliant color with a desert landscape as blazing red titles announced the beginning of the main movie. Matthew leaned back for the show but he glanced over where Nicodemus was sitting. Maybe Nicodemus went back for popcorn or a drink. But the seat was still empty. Nicodemus had left.

After the movie was over and the audience began to leave the theater, Matthew and Bernie stopped to look at the poster for the new movie that would be playing in a few days. It was a drama, a subject neither boy was interested in and their looks reflected a disappointment. "It's one of those movies where adults talk a lot and nothing happens," said Bernie, "I'll never understand why anyone would want to watch old people talking."

Hi Matthew, Hi Bernie," Stephanie's familiar voice spoke behind them. Matthew had been expecting this, knowing that Stephanie would take advantage of the fact that she was with her mother and that he and Bernie had to be nice. Mrs. Simpson was looking at the movie poster.

"Uh, Hi Stephanie," Matthew answered. Stephanie turned to Bernie, "Yeah, Hi," he mumbled.

"Did you see the previews of the new show with Natalie Wood?" Stephanie asked. Bernie nodded weakly, "Yeah."

"I think I look a lot like her, don't you?" Stephanie said, looking directly at Matthew, who suddenly felt like he was on the spot, like when Miss Major looked directly at him in class today when he told everyone about the Emperor of Mars. Now it was Stephanie who had that look and he wondered why girls could make him feel so scared of what he was going to say next.

"I don't know," Matthew uttered. A glance from Bernie gave him his next words, "Uh, we gotta go Stephanie, Bye." Matthew quickly turned and left with Bernie right behind him. Stephanie watched them go, feeling slighted and a little bit angry.

"All right, Stephanie, let's go home. You got to see your movie," Mrs. Simpson said. She had noticed the brief conversation and had also noticed Stephanie's sad look. It brought a smile to her although she discretely hid it from Stephanie.

The moment brought back memories that now had faded from her everyday life, warm and bittersweet memories of her youth and realizing that her little girl was now becoming her own person. Stephanie was beginning to experience love albeit a youthful and innocent one. Mrs. Simpson wasn't like her husband at all in fact she was known to be kind and friendly like Stephanie was.

"Mom, why do boys act like they don't even think you're alive?" Stephanie asked.

Mrs. Simpson thought for a moment, finding the right words seemed a little difficult. "Because we let them get away with too much," she answered.

Stephanie looked puzzled, "What do you mean?"

"You'll understand when you're older," Mrs. Simpson said. She took her daughter's hand and began to lead her away, "Let's go home."

Stephanie looked puzzled, "How come every time I ask you why, you say I'll understand when I'm older?"

"Because you will," Mrs. Simpson answered as they walked down the street.

11

Not far away and about the same time, Miss Major had decided to go for an evening walk after she had spent two hours marking papers for her class. The night was warm and she put a light sweater on over her blouse. Combined with a pair of jeans she looked more like a teenager than a schoolteacher.

Main Street was mostly empty, only a handful of cars around the café as she walked along. It was very quiet as it always was, somewhere a dog barked and it once again began a series of dogs barking until they all finally quit.

She laughed to herself, that was about all the life that was evident and for all purposes she imagined that she was the only person on Earth. It was a long way from the year she spent in the city at Teacher's College after she had graduated from high school.

The city was everything she had hoped for and she easily fell right into the nightlife and museums and the joy of life the young people she watched who seemed to pursue life so strongly.

She had even had a brief encounter with a handsome French student who she had met at the Museum. They would talk about many things while drinking coffee in small Italian cafes, something she wouldn't even dream of finding in her own home town. She decided then and there that one day she would go to Paris.

But here she was, working as a teacher in a little town not unlike her own and a sadness swept through her for a brief moment. She liked teaching and she liked the students but part of her wondered where her life would lead her. She wondered if she'd ever go to Paris, or if she would remain in a small town all her life. The men she met in small towns weren't as exciting as the men in the city. While they spoke of art and music and ideas the few men around here she had met spoke of tractors and whether it would rain and how soon should the crops be harvested.

Miss Major's walk had led her to the Crescent Cafe. She glanced inside to see several people either huddled into a booth or sitting at the counter. Then she entered.

Inside, the sound of people talking and music from the jukebox brought a warmness of companionship. It wasn't exactly the same as the Italian cafes in the city but it was close enough to offer some comfort on a quiet night.

Miss Major found a seat at the counter and when Sam walked up and asked her what she'd like she said that a coffee would do nicely. Sam nodded and went to get a cup of coffee for her. As she waited she looked around the café. There were three teens in a booth, she recognized them from school but didn't know their names as they were in high school and she had no real association with them. There was an older man dressed in overalls eating a hamburger and French fries with coffee at the same counter she sat at. He never looked around, satisfied to just eat his meal.

Then she noticed someone else in a booth by himself. It was Nicodemus, holding a cup of coffee in his hand, staring straight ahead. There was something odd about his look, he seemed almost to be in a trance of some kind. Miss Major turned away, thinking that her own stare would make him feel uneasy in that mysterious way that people seemed to sense when someone else was watching them. But was she watching him? Or was she just looking? She couldn't help but admit there was something about Nicodemus that she just couldn't quite understand. She had heard a few stories from the other teachers about how strange he had become since he had returned from the war. And she had learned that he had a wife who left town before he returned. And that he kept to himself.

She also noticed as others did that he had a very strong presence about him. You wanted to study him, she thought, you wanted to know more about him. He was still a good-looking man although he seemed to attempt to conceal any kind of style. He wore blue jeans and an old army jacket that was worn and frayed. Yet it suited him in a way she could not quite explain.

She could also feel some of the pain he had, a feeling of loss most likely from the loss of his family and probably from the war. She had seen soldiers come back from the war that had fallen into great depressions and led unhappy lives due to the experiences of war. Nicodemus had this but he also had something else. Something she could not quite put her finger on. He was different than most people, but in a way she didn't quite understand.

Suddenly Nicodemus snapped out of his trance and turned directly at her. It took Miss

Major a second to realize he was looking directly at her. And she was looking back. She gathered her senses and turned back to her coffee and then at the coffee machine and then the calendar on the wall, then back at her coffee as she sipped it. For a long moment she felt Nicodemus's intense look and it made her feel uncomfortable and maybe a little bit scared. But just as quickly as that feeling of being watched came it disappeared. Miss Major waited for a long while before she dared to glance back towards Nicodemus. When she finally did, he was gone. He had disappeared completely. She looked around the café, but there was no sign of him anywhere. It was like he was never really there.

Outside the café, Nicodemus stood in the shadows and watched Miss Major look around the café. After a moment, he turned and walked back towards the elevators, which again stood like ominous dark sentinels waiting. Then he saw them. The same lights as before, this time dancing around one of the elevators. Nobody else was on the street. Nicodemus looked up at the elevators again just long enough to see the lights shoot off into the dark sky. And he didn't know yet that there were two other people who noticed something about the elevators. Matthew and Stephanie.

12

Matthew didn't know his favorite teacher was out walking the streets of his little town this night. He was sitting on the rooftop of Bernie's dad's hotel. This was a favorite spot for Matthew and Bernie, a place where they could look out at the entire town as the hotel, except for the elevators, was the highest building in town.

Their view was a complete circle of the entire town which at 568 people wasn't really all that big. A single street in a big city could have more people living on it. And the view of the night sky was truly spectacular. But Matthew and Bernie had missed the lights that Nicodemus saw.

Right now the view of sky or the town wasn't what the two boys were looking at right now. With a flashlight's beam they both looked down at a Sears catalog where they studied the pages containing female models in colorful summer clothing and bathing suits and underwear. Their faces were serious, as though studying a subject from school.

"Her or her," Bernie said as he pointed to the models.

"You gotta pick one," Matthew answered.

Bernie paused, studied both models for a long second. "Her," he said. Matthew studied the models again.

Then, with calm expertise, he pointed at his choice.

"Her," Matthew spoke softly.

"You'd marry her?"

"That's what I said."

Bernie leaned back, thought for a minute. "I think they all look the same," he said.

Matthew shook his head, "Bernie, look at her, she's beautiful."

"Looks like Miss Major," Bernie smiled. Matthew reacted quickly, "Does not."

"Does too. Miss Major's too old for you to marry, anyway," Bernie challenged.

"When you get older, you catch up," Matthew reasoned.

Bernie thought for a minute then looked at the pictures again, "Nancy Carsen is my age. She's always real nice to me. 'Course you can never tell about those things because when people grow up they change. But I like her."

"You're supposed to love them," Matthew said.

"What's the difference?"

"Love is a bigger deal," Matthew answered. "It kinda hits you, like one day you're walking along the street and you fall in love. I think it's sorta like getting punched."

"That's only in the movies," Bernie supposed.

There was a moment of silence between them, neither really knew the mystery of love, or at least wanted to offer their theories, after all they were only twelve years old. Instead, Matthew leaned back and looked up at the sky. Bernie joined him and they both gazed into the beginning of a full starry night. Somehow it made them more relaxed.

"I'd like to marry Nancy," Bernie said, "But I don't think I could. She's not Jewish."

Still looking up at the sky, Matthew said, "That doesn't matter. Old Mr. Kerkopovitch married an Indian lady."

Bernie shook his head, "It's different. You don't know what it's like to be Jewish."

"Sometimes I think that maybe everybody thinks that nobody knows what it's like to be them," Matthew offered back. Bernie pondered on that for a moment.

"Yeah. Maybe," he said back.

Matthew didn't answer this time instead he focused his look on something far off. Bernie noticed him. "What are you looking at?" he asked. Matthew was looking at the elevators. "What is it?"

The thought had come to Matthew in a quiet second and it flowed into his mind almost like a voice calling him. "Let's go see what landed on Nicodemus's field," Matthew said.

"Oh no," Bernie shot back, "I'm not going there. It's after dark and my parents will kill me."

Matthew was now on a mission, his mind was made up and he knew how to convince Bernie he was right. "Okay, if you're scared you don't have to go."

This was now an official dare. Maybe a double dare. In a twelve-year old's world this was serious stuff, life-changing decisions were made on dares and double-dares were even more important. If word got out that someone failed to act on a double dare it could spell doom. In short Bernie now had few options.

The elevators were all dark except for a yard light that spilled a circle of light beneath it. The two boys stuck to the shadows of the tall buildings and inched their way towards

Nicodemus's shack and the wheat field beyond it.

"Where's his dog?" Bernie whispered.

"He'll be sleeping,' Matthew supposed, "He's old."

Matthew stepped through the fence that separated the wheat field from the elevator property. Bernie waited as he collected some courage then he too slipped through the fence. Both boys hunched down, breathing hard, their hearts trembled with excitement.

"Let's leave." Bernie said.

"We're almost there," Matthew answered.

"I don't care," Bernie returned, "let's leave."

Just then there was a scuffle in the shadows behind them followed by a low growl. "It's him," Bernie nearly shouted.

While Matthew had led this little adventure suddenly he felt his fears growing. He strained to see in the dark when suddenly Nicodemus's dog barked out loud. As always a handful of barks returned from other dogs in town.

"Run!" Bernie shouted.

Both boys ran back to the fence, climbing through as fast as they can as the barking came closer. Bernie stumbled at the fence and Matthew turned back and helped his friend through. The barking was closer and closer and they both fell, tripping on a fence post and falling to the ground. As they struggled to get up a strong beam of light fell on them. The two boys froze.

"What are you boys doing here?" a familiar voice shouted.

Bernie could not speak, Matthew searched for words as he stared into the glaring light. "Nothing... we... we're lost," he said weakly.

The flashlight lowered a little, just enough for Matthew and Bernie to make out Nicodemus. "You boys come here," he said is a gruff voice.

"Run, Matthew, run!" Bernie shouted.

Both boys rolled away and leapt to their feet running in two different directions. Within seconds they disappeared out of the flashlight's beam.

Nicodemus shook his head and then shouted, "It's dangerous here at night. I said keep away!" Then he crossed over to an old rocking chair on the porch of his shack. He sat down.

The old dog came panting up, found his spot on an old rug, turned around twice and then lay down quietly. Nicodemus reached for an old .303 Enfield army rifle and straddled it across his lap.

He had acquired the rifle from a farmer who had moved away. At first he really didn't want it as the weapon brought back memories of the war. It leaned against a corner for a long time and each time he passed it he would contemplate throwing it away. But then someone could find it and possibly hurt themselves.

He knew all too well what a rifle could do and he was responsible enough to avoid any accidents. So he decided to keep it there for now.

The night was particularly silent and it brought back memories to Nicodemus of another time. After the war he hand wandered across the country hitchhiking to the west coast and back. He avoided coming back to his home town for the longest time and when he finally did, he knew it would not be good. For one thing it wasn't Empire.

The town that once sat on the top of Thunder Hill was gone, just a few wooden buildings aging in the ever-present wind that blew across the top of the mountain. There was no message left for him, no sign that anyone had been there for a few years.

His own home had long fallen apart and there was no sign of his wife Mary. She had written to him when he was in Europe but when the war ended, Nicodemus found himself unsure of what to do. He would have strange memory lapses; he'd remember a face, but not a name. Doctors said it was shell-shock and they had no cure. They gave him pills but he didn't like how they made him ill so he stopped taking them.

Still, there was something about the town that was no more and he had a feeling that he needed to stay nearby. For one thing the recent flashes of memory he had been experiencing would continue to lead him to believe that something would happen. He just wasn't sure what it would be.

Nicodemus set the rifle down as he looked upwards at the elevators rising into the darkness. Beyond it was the star-filled night sky. He wondered about the lights he had seen that night or at least he thought he had seen. He wasn't even sure why he held the rifle nearby except that a feeling had come over him, something that was going to happen soon, something big. The flashes of memory seemed to say someone was coming. Someone he knew.

On Main Street the boys finally stopped to catch their breath. Nobody was chasing them as they rested.

"Come on," Bernie said, "Let's go home."

Matthew looked back at the elevators. "Did you see, he was waiting for something?"

"I don't know. Let's go, okay?"

"There is something there, Bernie."

"I'm going home," Bernie answered as he started to walk down the middle of Main Street. Matthew looked back once and then turned to follow Bernie. At that moment a distant roll of thunder echoed across the night sky. It made Matthew stop as he looked up just in time to see a distant lightning bolt light up the sky for a precious second or two.

The distant thunder was also noticed by Nicodemus on his porch. He held the rifle tightly as he looked towards a bolt of lightning that briefly illuminated Thunder Hill several miles from town. The dog growled. Nicodemus looked down at the dog.

Easy, Dog," he said softly, "It's all right. Nothing's going to happen. Not yet. You'll know when."

The dog settled down but Nicodemus never loosened the grip on his rifle as he watched the distant lightning.

13

Sam Wong opened his cafe bright and early as he had done for twenty years. Usually there were a few farmers hanging around waiting, ready for an early breakfast. They were mostly the unmarried men who didn't have a wife to cook for them. Sometimes they just wanted an hour or so to catch up on the local gossip. But today was different as a strange buzzing sound caused Sam to look down the street where he saw something he could not believe. At the same time a brilliant light blinded him.

There, on Main Street, an alien life-form emerged from the light.

It was pure evil, dripping green slime, with blood-filled eyeballs and tentacles that oozed filth and destruction. And it had Tommy's face. The creature undulated towards Sam and, in a split-second wrapped itself around him and swallowed him whole.

A lone figure ran up to the café. It was Miss Major. Behind her the town laid in waste, buildings burning, spaceships flying over it. Yet there was just something odd about everything. It was as though the background was painted, like in a 1950's movie filmed on a studio lot. Tommy the alien turned and saw Miss Major. He slobbered towards her, his dripping tentacles swinging around in big circles as he came closer.

"Don't touch her," a voice commanded.

It was Matthew, armed with his BB gun. He stepped onto Main Street, aimed and fired. The gun's copper BBs bounced off Tommy. Matthew kept firing until he realized that his gun was useless. Almost every boy in town had a BB gun, it was standard issue and was used primarily for shooting at cans, cardboard targets and sometimes bottles, although you got into trouble if you broke bottles.

As Tommy came closer to Miss Major, she turned to Matthew and screamed for help. But Matthew was helpless as he watched Tommy approach with his oozing tentacles reaching out for her. Matthew was frantic and he threw his gun at Tommy which did little more than bounce off Tommy's alien skin. Suddenly a wind rushed down the street creating dust devils as it moved towards Matthew, Miss Major and Tommy. The wind blasted into Tommy sending his alien body tumbling backwards down the street towards the elevators in a cloud of dust until he disappeared.

Matthew wiped his eyes clean and looked behind him. There standing at least ten feet tall was Nicodemus. He had a strange glow that seemed to be moving around his entire body with little sparks that bubbled. He began to walk towards Matthew. Suddenly Matthew felt afraid and he stepped back away from Nicodemus.

But just as he moved back he bumped into something soft and sticky. Matthew turned to face Tommy the alien back from his tumbled state and now wrapping his tentacles around Matthew.

Matthew shouted as loud as he could as he tried to reach for Nicodemus who reached out for him but was himself pulled back and away from Matthew. As Matthew struggled the light around him turned into a rainbow of colors and he began spinning around and around as he struggled to free himself from Tommy's tentacles.

"Matthew," a voice cried, "Matthew, wake up. Wake up!"

Matthew opened his eyes and realized he was looking at his mother. He was in his bed safe and sound. It took only a second to realize he was dreaming. Morning light streamed into his window.

"What was it?" Elana held him.

"The Martian," Matthew managed to say.

Elana just shook her head, "There are no Martians here, only us. You have school."

Matthew leaned back as Elana stroked his hair and kissed him on the forehead. "It's those movies you see, Matthew, that's all. Maybe you should not see so many. Now get up and I'll have breakfast for you."

Elana left the room and Matthew lay there for a moment trying to make sense of the dream. Why was Tommy a monster, and why did Nicodemus rescue him and Miss Major? And where did Miss Major go to? But it was too many questions for so early in the morning and Matthew looked out the window again just to make sure that things were still normal. But he was in for a surprise.

Bernie was already waiting near the school gate as Matthew approached. He paced nervously as he greeted Matthew.

"Did you hear?" Bernie asked Matthew.

"What?"

"Dolores Anderson."

"What about her?"

Bernie paused and took a deep breath. Looking around he leaned towards Matthew. "Her mom saw a flying saucer. It crashed into her house."

Matthew looked at Bernie, "Don't kid me today, okay?"

"I'm not kidding," Bernie answered.

Dolores Anderson, all of ten years old and in pigtails, was telling her story for the seventh time as Matthew and Bernie approached her. There was a handful of kids standing around her listening intently.

Dolores was the daughter of Anderson, the man who had seen what Nicodemus had seen in the wheat field. She and her parents lived on a farm near town where he grew wheat and raised a few cows and chickens. Dolores had always enjoyed attention and had a flare for the dramatic as she told her story.

"And so she was finishing the breakfast dishes and looked out the window and a light shined in her eyes," Dolores spun, "kinda like a mirror reflecting the sun. It was so bright it nearly blinded her."

Matthew leaned in closely pushing a few Grade Ones out of his way. This was his story as much as hers and he was not going to take a back seat.

Dolores continued, "Suddenly there was a screaming sound, and the roof of our kitchen exploded and a spaceship crashed through the whole kitchen right into the floor and into the ground. Mom ran outside screaming, we were in the barn when it happened."

Matthew interrupted, "What happened?"

"I'm coming to that Matthew," Dolores smiled sarcastically. She paused for maximum effect, watching the eyes of the kids surrounding her. She waited for just the right time.

"We don't know. By the time we came out, it was gone. All except the hole in our roof and floor," Dolores said.

This wasn't enough for Matthew. "What about the spaceship, is it under your house".

"I don't know," Dolores sighed, "I had to go to school".

Bernie stepped in, "That's a dopey story, Dolores."

Dolores glared at him, "No it's not. My mom saw it and she said it was a spaceship."

"She was just dreaming it," Bernie said.

"You can say what you want," Dolores glared, "I don't care. It's true."

"How do you know it's true?" Matthew said.

"Because I saw a whole bunch of grown-ups at Nicodemus's this morning and they were walking through his field," Dolores smiled knowing that Matthew couldn't top that piece of information. "And there was a big burned circle there, right in the middle of the field." In truth, she really had seen a handful of local men walking through the wheat field like they were looking for something. And her father had acted very peculiar when her mother had come screaming out of the kitchen. It was like he wasn't all that surprised yet he seemed a little bit scared, something she had never seen in her father before.

And then there was the huge hole in their roof and floor.

"So?" Matthew shot back.

"So you know what happened at Nicodemus's place, don't you?" Dolores replied.

As the other kids watched with anticipation for the next challenge Dolores saved the best for last.

"A flying saucer landed there," she said, "My dad said so. I heard him tell my mom when they didn't know I was listening."

Matthew turned towards the grain elevators as the school bell rang and the other kids began to head for the doors. But Matthew wasn't following.

"I gotta go there," Matthew answered.

"You're gonna be late for school," Bernie said.

"I have to go," Matthew turned towards the street.

"You're gonna get in trouble, big trouble," was Bernie's answer. But Matthew was already running down the street towards the elevators.

"Miss Major's gonna ask," Bernie shouted. But Matthew was already too far away to hear.

14

Nobody was standing in the field when Matthew arrived at Nicodemus's house. But he really couldn't see the whole field and he for sure couldn't see where the field had a circle burned into it. But someone had already seen Matthew as he heard the undeniable growl. The dog. Matthew froze.

The dog continued growling as it approached Matthew. He knew it was already too late to run. He also remembered the priest at church talking about miracles and how they would happen to save people. If there were miracles this would be a good time to have one.

The dog snarled a little as he came up to Matthew. Running now would most certainly be a bad idea. Then, Matthew had an idea. He let one hand hang down slowly near the dog. It snarled. Matthew closed his eyes.

Then the dog did a dog thing. It raised its head to Matthew's now outstretched hand and smelled it. The dog's dark cold nose touched

Matthew's hand and left a thin layer of dog slime. In the moment that followed, Matthew waited. The growling stopped. There was silence. Matthew still didn't dare to open his eyes. There was another thrust of cold nose into Matthew's hand. No teeth, no growling. Slowly he opened his eyes. At his side the dog sat quietly watching him.

"Good boy," was the best Matthew could come up with. The dog's tail wagged a little. Matthew extended his hand ever so slowly moving just over the dog's head.

"Thata boy," Matthew said softly. His hand patted the dog that now was his new friend. "What's out there, boy, huh, what's there?" Matthew asked.

As if to answer, the dog stared towards the field as though he really knew why Matthew was there. From here Matthew barely made out Nicodemus, standing waist-high in the wheat. He moved out of sight.

Matthew wasn't sure what to do. He would be risking Nicodemus's anger if he revealed himself. And he wasn't sure what the man would do. He wasn't even sure if the dog would still be quiet or leap at him. That's when he saw the ladder leaning against the house. It reached to the roof.

The ladder like the house was old and rickety. Even Matthew's light weight creaked on the first rung as he began to climb up. He looked back at the dog who just watched. It was almost as though he was waiting for Matthew to fall. Maybe then he'd charge at him, Matthew thought.

Matthew took another step and another. One rung creaked too dangerously and Matthew stepped over it onto the next one. He soon was at the edge of the roof and he slowly took the last two rungs and stepped gingerly onto the roof. He looked down once and a shudder ran though him as the distance to the ground was certainly enough to hurt him if he fell. Then he remembered why he was there.

Matthew slowly stepped up the angled roof towards the peak. The roof itself cracked and creaked and he hoped it wouldn't cave in until he saw what he came to see. As he reached the peak he slowly raised his head over it and looked down at the field before him.

He could not believe his eyes.

There beneath him, the field was perfectly normal except for one thing. One big thing. There was a perfectly round circle where the wheat had been flattened to the ground, each stalk having been pushed down by some immense weight, each stalk curved into a circle. The circle was about thirty feet in diameter and immaculately cut sharp at the edges.

Whatever or whomever did this did an artistic job of it. And that wasn't all. There was also what appeared to be burn marks within the circle. They reminded Matthew of coffee cup rings that were left on a tabletop. And there was the slight scent of something having been burned. But before Matthew could reason out what he was looking at a voice shouted.

"You, boy! Get down!"

Matthew snapped back to reality. He saw Nicodemus leaving the circle and coming towards him from the field. He turned too quickly and fell backwards and began sliding down the roof towards the edge and beyond that to the ground. For a second he had a flash of the dog waiting with fangs bared. But he didn't have to worry because he would never get that far.

Just as he regained his balance a sickening CRACK ripped through the air. The sound of wood splintering and breaking under Matthew gave him a flash of what was about to happen. In that precious second before it did Matthew already felt the pain of falling. All it took was the roof giving way and collapsing on the spot where he stood. He went crashing down through wood and dust and everything became a blur as he felt the first jab at his arm of something that felt like a wooden beam.

In that moment, all Matthew could see was dust and wood and sun and then blackness for what seemed forever.

"Are you okay?"

Matthew opened his eyes. Where was he, was he alive, what happened to him? These were the first things that occurred to him as the brightness of the sun shone on him. Slowly it all came back. He was on the roof and he must have fallen through. But where was he and whose voice was asking him if he was okay?

"I said, are you all right?" The voice asked again.

Matthew's brain checked for pain. There was a dull ache in his side and a bit of dizziness in his eyes. But that was all. Of course he wasn't sure if he could stand up. "I… I think so," Matthew answered.

He still didn't see whoever it was who was asking him. It wasn't his mother, and it wasn't Miss Major. Then he remembered it was Nicodemus. Matthew's eyes focused above him and Nicodemus became sharp and clear standing over him.

"This house is too old to walk on, you oughtta know better," Nicodemus said, "Can you stand up?"

Matthew coordinated his brain slowly and found the strength to try standing up. Slowly, he rose to his knees and then to one foot. An arm grabbed his arm to help him and Matthew slowly stood upright.

"Just stand still for a minute, boy," Nicodemus said. His grip on Matthew's arm was strong but not menacing. Matthew looked around and realized he was on the porch of the shack. He looked up at the roof.

"I fell," Matthew said slowly, "I... I'm sorry."

Nicodemus took his grip off Matthew and stepped back. "You should be, I have to repair that now," he answered, "Why'd you climb that damn old ladder?"

Matthew's senses were coming back. Except for a bruise on his arm and some scratches he was okay. And then there was the question that continued to burn in his mind. "What made the circles?" Matthew said quietly.

Nicodemus glanced back at the field and it seemed as though he was looking for words to explain. "You best go now," was all he said.

"It was a flying saucer, wasn't it?" Matthew tried again. Nicodemus didn't answer, he just looked away. "Are they going to come back?" Matthew pressed.

Nicodemus turned back to Matthew looking very serious. Matthew knew he wasn't angry like he usually was. In fact this was the first time Matthew had heard Nicodemus talking in a normal tone. It wasn't anger, it seemed more like he didn't want to talk about the circle out in the field.

"Nothing was here," was all Nicodemus said.

"I just want to see," Matthew pleaded, "I won't ask about it anymore. Just let me see what's there."

Nicodemus began to walk away from Matthew. Matthew walked behind him. Each step gave him new courage until he stopped in his tracks. "You gotta. I'm gonna come back again even if you don't let me, I'm gonna come back again and again."

This time Nicodemus stopped and turned to Matthew. He studied him for a moment, and Matthew began to see a different side of Nicodemus. He didn't seem mad or scary or anything like the kids in town had said he was. He looked like a real person. Nicodemus was thinking about letting him see the circle. Matthew couldn't explain it, but he knew that was what Nicodemus was thinking. He was going to see the circle.

As Nicodemus led him Matthew closed his eyes and stepped into the crop circle with delicate steps almost expecting anything to happen.

He could feel the wheat brush his pants until suddenly he was in the open. He slowly opened his eyes and found himself right in the middle of the circle. Matthew wanted suddenly to run, to make a mad dash for the safety of the wheat that surrounded the circle. But something else told him to wait.

"What is it?" Matthew asked.

Nicodemus looked as well, "They said it was the wind, or electricity spinning around," he answered, then added, "or cows walking in a circle."

Matthew knelt down and touched the pushed down wheat stalks and felt the texture. He raised his hand to his nose, it smelled like burnt wood. Like someone had set fire to it. But yet, it was only the wheat that lay beaten down that was charred.

None of the standing wheat around the circle had even been touched. A fire wouldn't burn in a circle by itself and not burn the rest of the field.

"What do you think it is?" Matthew asked.

Nicodemus was still looking away, towards the distant horizon where clouds were forming over Thunder Hill. He wasn't sure how to answer Matthew, he wasn't even sure himself. He certainly couldn't tell the boy that this may be a message, that somebody or something was coming. There were enough people in town who thought he was crazy and he didn't need any more suspicion.

And then there was another thought that crossed his mind. He wasn't sure if this was a good thing or a bad thing or even if it was anything at all.

He had seen wheat fields pressed down before. A good wind would do that and a hail storm would do even more damage. And the burn marks could have been caused by lightning.

In fact, it was easy to explain, he figured. But then why did he have the feeling it would be more than just the wind or hail or lightning. That was something he couldn't answer even to the boy. But there was one thing that Nicodemus could say that could most likely strike fear in him. Nicodemus looked straight at Matthew and, with a dead serious look, spoke slowly.

"I think you should be at school," was all he said.

Matthew froze as it all came back to him. He looked at his Gene Autry watch. It was after two and he wasn't at his desk.

15

The schoolyard was empty as Matthew sped past the gate, running as fast as his heart could push him. He had committed the greatest crime a kid could commit. He had skipped out of school. There were stories about kids who skipped school and some of them ran through his mind as he ran to the front door.

Legend had it that Oliver Wachkin had been sent to jail or at least, some kind of reform school for six months when he constantly skipped school. There were the stories of parents who punished kids by not having their birthday party and worse gave no gifts at Christmas. But the only punishment that Matthew feared the most, the thing that could ruin his entire life was that Miss Major would want nothing to do with him ever again.

He had betrayed her trust. Matthew's mind ran through a score of excuses, each not good enough or imaginative enough to be very convincing.

Matthew's hand gripped the door handle and twisted it open. Except it didn't open. He stumbled with the handle again. It still didn't open. Something was wrong. His mind ran through possibilities, were they deliberately keeping him out? Was this his punishment? Would Miss Major ever talk to him again?

"School's closed," a voice spoke.

Matthew looked around to find the source. He didn't quite know what the voice said, but he knew who it was. His eyes fell on Paul, his classmate, who was tossing a worn tennis ball that he had found against the wide brick wall of the school. "Had a flood in the basement," Paul added, as he continued tossing the tennis ball, catching it on the rebound.

Matthew couldn't believe it. This may have been his salvation. A flood in the basement. It wasn't new, the old pipes in the water system flooded at least twice a year, sometimes in winter when once, the entire basement floor was once frozen over like a skating rink.

But now it was a life saver. Or at least so it seemed. There was still one burning question but before Matthew could ask, Paul was already ahead of him. "Miss Major was asking where you were," Paul shrugged, then smiled, "You're in trouble." Matthew's salvation had worked for a few minutes but life wasn't always so perfect. Now he had to face a greater fear and he knew what must be done.

Matthew walked slowly towards Mrs. Jenkins's house. A passerby would have seen Matthew's look of despair and fear and figured him waiting for his own execution. As Matthew reached the door he had a moment of clarity. Was he doing the right thing? Should he just go home and wait until tomorrow morning. What if his mother knew, but what if Miss Major hadn't had time to tell her? She was working anyways and wouldn't be home for at least two hours.

His answer came when the door opened and Mrs. Jenkins stared out at him, surprised. While she had seen Matthew in town she didn't know his name and so she smiled. Matthew thought that if she knew why he was here she most certainly would not be smiling.

"Hello," Mrs. Jenkins said pleasantly, "what can I do for you, young man?"

Matthew searched for the courage he would need to answer her. In what seemed like a million seconds, but more like a heartbeat, Matthew stuttered, "I... I came to see Miss Major."

Miss Jenkins led Matthew into her house and up the steps where she knocked on the door.

After what seemed an eternity for Matthew Miss Major's voice spoke, "Come in". Miss Jenkins opened the door to Miss Major's upstairs apartment. Matthew glanced inside where sunshine streamed through light curtains and a slight breeze created by the open door passed over him. But there was no sign of Miss Major.

"Come in, Matthew," her voice spoke from somewhere inside. It sounded pleasant enough but there was a different tone to it. Matthew could not get it down yet but it was almost like another voice that she was using. It was her but it didn't quite sound like her.

Mrs. Jenkins pushed him gently inside.

"Thank you, Mrs. Jenkins," Miss Major added. Mrs. Jenkins smiled and slowly closed the door behind her. Matthew stood perfectly still as his eyes took in the apartment. The place was airy and cheerful; there was a small sofa that was pushed against one wall that was lower due to the angled ceiling just above it. Someone could sit on the sofa but had to be careful not to stand up too fast as they could bump their head on the angle. To the right there was a narrow doorway that led to what looked like a bedroom.

Near the window where the sun shone through sat a small kitchen table and two chairs.

Matthew wondered why she would have two chairs seeing as she wasn't married, didn't have any kids, and wasn't ever seen with a man. He didn't like the thought of a man up here sitting at that table.

"Can you help me for a minute," Miss Major said as she appeared holding a large limited edition poster print of what looked like two men playing cards. "Do you like it," Miss Major asked, smiling, "It's called The Card Players, and it was done by a French impressionist painter called Paul Cezanne."

But Matthew's eyes weren't on the Card Players. He was looking at Miss Major. She was dressed in blue jeans and a red plaid men's workshirt and her hair was tied back in a pony tail. It was hard to believe this was the same person who was a school teacher. Matthew had seen his other teachers on the street and they dressed and looked pretty much like they did in school. This was different. If you didn't know you could have thought she was one of the students. Not in Grade 6 of course but high school, definitely.

It was like he had stepped into another world. The old rules didn't seem to apply here in her own personal world. She was just a girl now, still pretty and still a teacher, but also a girl like the teenagers in Grade Twelve. It struck him how young she really was. Miss Levitt, his first grade teacher was never a girl as far as Matthew was concerned. She was always an adult and she always wore frumpy dresses that made her look like she was really old. But right now the pretty girl was looking at him. And Matthew knew exactly why.

"I... I'm sorry I wasn't at school today, Miss Major," he stumbled.

Miss Major studied him for what seemed like a long time but was only a few seconds. Matthew stood still, ready for whatever would be coming from her. She might be a pretty girl right now but tomorrow she would be a teacher again. And teachers were not usually friends.

"I need some tacks," she said as she stretched the print against the wall, "there's some in the drawer in the drawer by the window."

Matthew nodded and turned to locate the drawer. It was by the window like she said and he walked slowly towards it. Miss Major began locating the perfect spot on the wall for the poster.

"Mrs. Jenkins said she doesn't mind putting a few into these old walls especially for something so pretty, don't you think?"

Matthew nodded as he reached the set of drawers and opened the top one. Inside, neatly folded, were women's garments, like the kind Bernie and he had seen before in the catalog. He wasn't sure what to do, there surely would be no tacks here. He turned to Miss Major but she was busy raising the poster and couldn't see him.

"Did you find them?"

Matthew delicately reached around for the tacks. He thought it an odd place for them but couldn't see any tacks.

"I think they're in that little box on top," Miss Major said as the poster folded over her head. She struggled to push it back without making fold marks. Matthew glanced on the top of the drawers and saw a little box. He closed the drawer and reached for the box and opened it. The tacks were inside.

"I got them," Matthew said, relieved. He carried the tacks over to her as she finally right-sided the poster. With one hand bracing the top and the other pressing in the bottom Miss Major held the poster in place.

"You can pin the corners," she said without looking at him.

Matthew leaned forward, realizing he had to sneak in under her arms to reach the other corners. He held his breath as he reached under, barely brushing against her waist, just enough to feel the touch of her shirt. He pressed the pin into the poster, sticking it to the wall.

"Great, now the other sides," she said. Matthew didn't have to get too close to her to fasten the other tacks and so he carried out the job a little slower than it really took. For a second, he caught scent of something like wild flowers. It took him a few more seconds to realize it was perfume, that thing that women poured onto themselves to smell nice. Even his mother had perfume although she rarely wore it.

And now he had stolen a whiff of Miss Major's perfume. Bernie would never believe this, Matthew thought quietly.

When the poster was on the wall, Miss Major stood back to look at it. At first she smiled but slowly the smile seemed to dissolve.

"This might be the closest I get to Paris," she said, and the words seemed to sound sad to Matthew. He knew about Paris.

"I saw a movie about Paris once," he said in an authoritative tone. He didn't mention that it was one of those love story movies that he really didn't care for. She would probably have liked it.

"Yes, so did I," she answered, "a couple of them." After I graduated from Teacher's school I was going to go there."

"You were going to go to Paris," he asked, "the real Paris?"

"My big adventure," Miss Major answered, "I'm afraid I didn't go."

"Why are you afraid?" Matthew asked.

"It's a figure of speech, Matthew," she smiled, "I meant it was probably going to be my only big adventure, you know, see something else besides a small town."

"Why didn't you go?" Matthew asked.

Miss Major seemed to stop and think about that for awhile. There was an awkward silence until she returned from whatever world she had temporarily disappeared into. "Sometimes, things don't work out the way you want," she said quietly.

Her smile came back again and she was happy again.

"Maybe you'll go back someday," Matthew said suddenly, "It's not as far away as Mars."

Miss Major turned to him and smiled, "You're right," she said. Then her smile turned to something more serious. "Where were you today, Matthew?" she asked. And suddenly her voice was a school teacher's voice.

Matthew knew it would eventually lead to this and he already had burned the previous moments of pure joy into his memory. Now it was time to face the punishment.

"Well, Nicodemus, uh, Mr. Johnson, he kinda watches the grain elevators," Matthew started, "He's got this wheat field right behind them and..."

Matthew couldn't help but notice her reaction when he said Nicodemus's name. He wasn't sure what kind of reaction, but her manner changed for a brief moment, as though his name meant something to her or held interest.

It made Matthew curious and it also gave him a precious moment of his own where he had the advantage. With luck he might distract her totally.

"Something was there," Matthew said, trying to look dramatic. "It left a big circle right in his field and there were marks like from a huge flying saucer."

Miss Major had already recovered from her reaction. She had hoped it hadn't been too obvious to Matthew or to anyone for that matter. She wasn't even sure why it caused a reaction except that there was something about Nicodemus that challenged her ability to figure out what people were like. She wasn't able to pin him down, at least not yet.

"Really," she answered, realizing that wasn't much of an answer at all. It was time to change the subject as she faced Matthew with a more serious look. That teacher look. "Matthew, I think there's a lot of things we don't know about, but I don't think there's Martians hanging around Empire... or anywhere else," she said, changing to her teacher voice. "You missed some assignments. I can give them to you now."

Matthew hoped this would be as bad as it would get.

"I'll do them," he pleaded, "Honest."

Miss Major wasn't through as she continued, "That's not all. You're my responsibility during the school day Matthew. I didn't know where you were and I was concerned about you. I had to call your mother."

Matthew's eyes fell to the floor, she had called. As if life wasn't bad enough already now he would have to deal with his mother. And that meant one thing for sure. No movies for maybe two weeks.

Once she had forbidden him to go for two weeks but he had quietly seen two movies without her knowing it as Saturday movies sometimes had a matinee in the afternoon. Still this would interfere with Nicodemus and the Emperor of Mars.

"This flying saucer thing, well, you'd do better to think about real things, like school," Miss Major continued, "And you shouldn't be bothering Mr. Johnson."

Properly punished, Matthew shrugged. It was worth it having been with her.

Yes, Miss Major," he answered in a polite student tone. They might be teacher and student again, but the previous minutes with her would never go away. Then just as suddenly as she became teacher she smiled and Miss Major the girl came back. For a brief second a few strands of hair fell in her face and she brushed them back with her hand.

For Matthew it was the end of an almost perfect day.

16

After dinner Matthew ran out of the house and made a beeline straight for Bernie's parent's hotel. He ran down the near empty Main Street where only a car and two trucks were parked in front of the café. It took him less than a few minutes to reach the hotel and he went into the main entrance.

There was nobody at the check-in counter but that was pretty normal for early evenings. Besides the hotel rarely had more than a few people staying there. There were only ten small rooms and the guests were usually traveling salesmen and sometimes a family on vacation. Matthew ran up to the second floor and into a long hallway. There was nobody in the hallway as he ran to the very end.

It was here that Bernie and his parents made their home. Unlike other families in town, their home consisted of several hotel rooms, two of which were rebuilt into a kitchen and dining room. The rooms on the opposite side had been converted into a small living room and two bedrooms. Matthew had always liked this place, maybe because it was so different than regular homes. He thought it would be interesting to live in a hotel where people came from far away and stayed for a night and then left. Someday he just might stay at a hotel in a faraway town that he'd never been to. That wouldn't be hard because he'd never really been out of Empire except once for a funeral. But that was only about twenty miles away. Matthew poked his head into the living room.

Mrs. Bernstein was sitting on a sofa reading a book. She was different than most moms, he'd never seen other moms reading books. In fact, except for school, he'd never seen anyone in Empire reading books. She looked up from her book at him.

"Where's Bernie, Mrs. Bernstein?" Matthew asked.

"Bernie is with his father on the roof," she answered. She had a tiny bit of a smile on her face, knowing full well why Matthew was here right now. "Go, have a look," she added in a way that suggested something mysterious. But Matthew was already gone. "Be careful of the ladder, Matthew," she said even as a slamming door told her he never heard the words. She smiled to herself. Something big was going on up there.

Outside, Matthew began climbing the metal fire escape ladder that led up to the flat roof. The ladder went over the railing and down a few steps to the flat roof. He stepped down and was caught immediately by a view of the setting sun and the orange horizon. From here he could see most of the entire town.

But it was something he had seen a thousand times and now he was more interested in Bernie and his father. They were near the middle of the roof grappling with something that resembled a metal tower. It was a television antenna, an aluminum pole about eight feet tall with several shorter poles horizontally crossing at the top. The antenna pulled in the same signal as Simpson's store received. Bernie turned to see Matthew. "Come here, quick," he shouted.

Matthew lost no time in running across the roof. He joined Bernie and his father as they attempted to raise the antenna. "The TV came this afternoon," Bernie said breathlessly, "Right from the catalog."

Mr. Bernstein tried to balance the antenna but clearly was having problems. He was a soft-spoken man and Matthew had never heard him raise his voice to Bernie or anyone else. He was one of the local businessmen but he never seemed to join the others in any business functions. When they had their summer parade, nearly every businessman in town had a float or a sign, but Mr. Bernstein never seemed to bother with any displays. And since Bernie was his best friend Mr. Bernstein was the only father that Matthew had ever known close up. He had always found Bernie's family interesting because they didn't seem to do the same things as most people did in town. They would attend town events and even sit with others and talk, but they seemed to be different.

Matthew had heard Mr. Simpson talk about Mr. Bernstein once but he wasn't really sure what Mr. Simpson was trying to say. Whatever it was it probably wasn't nice. Mr. Simpson wasn't a very nice person. Again he wondered how Stephanie was his daughter. She was a bother sometimes, but she wasn't mean like him and Tommy.

"As long as you're here, Matthew, you can help us," Mr. Bernstein spoke.

"Sure," Matthew answered. There was no invitation needed as Matthew ran to them. "Is it going to be on soon?" he asked.

"We have to connect the antenna first," Bernie said with pride, "That's how it works."

Then he added, "The TV's an RCA Victor and it cost three hundred and nine dollars." Matthew couldn't imagine spending that much money.

Mr. Bernstein instructed the boys to hold the antenna straight up as he began to bolt in the base onto a block of wood hammered into the roof.

"Can I stay to watch it?" Matthew asked.

Mr. Bernstein smiled as he secured the antenna, "Oh, I suppose you can. But only until eight then your mother will want you home."

Matthew was beside himself, he was going to watch a TV and it wasn't in Mr. Simpson's store. That meant no more being scared of getting kicked out. Mr. Bernstein finished tightening the bolts and stood up. They all looked at the magnificent antenna and Mr. Bernstein pushed the antenna several times. It seemed to be solid.

"Now, you boys can go downstairs and get ready to turn it on," Mr. Bernstein said. Bernie and Matthew looked at each other with excitement in their eyes. They started to run back to the fire escape ladder.

"Boys," Mr. Bernstein spoke loudly, or as loud as Matthew had ever heard him. Both he and Bernie stopped.

"Walk, please," Mr. Bernstein said, "Don't run. I don't want anyone falling off the roof."

They slowed to a walk, still excited. Bernie thought of something as they reached the fire escape ladder. "Miss Major called your mom," he said, "Did you get the strap?"

Matthew looked at him. The strap was feared by every student in school. Matthew had never seen anyone getting it but stories abounded about the poor kid who was given the strap across his hands for disobeying a teacher or doing some horrible thing. It was a piece of heavy stiff leather and was kept in some secret place in every teacher's desk. And even the mention of it scared most of the smaller kids. Matthew had noticed that high schoolers weren't as scared and figured they must be too old for it.

No," was all he said with uncertainty. Who knew what tomorrow would bring. After all he did miss a half day of school. But something in him said that Miss Major wasn't the kind who liked to give kids the strap. In fact he doubted she even had one.

"What are you going to tell Miss Major tomorrow?" Bernie shot back.

"I talked to her already," Matthew answered with smugness in his voice.

"Where'd you see her?"

"At her place."

Bernie froze, "Her place?" he said unbelieving.

"Yeah, I helped her put up a picture," Matthew smiled casually like it was a normal event.

Bernie was in awe, "Wow! I never went to see a teacher at their place," he said, "I don't think I'd want to. What's it look like?"

"Like anyplace," Matthew said "And the picture is of two guys playing cards," he added, "It's from France."

Bernie grabbed Matthew and looked dead serious into his eyes.

"Does this mean you don't have to do homework anymore?" he asked, his eyes wide and anticipating an answer.

"Don't be dumb," Matthew answered, "We're just friends, is all."

Bernie stood there in the cooling purple light of the horizon and shook his head.

"Wow. A TV set and a guy who's friends with a teacher. What a day."

As Bernie climbed down the fire escape Matthew stopped and looked out towards the darkening town. It took a few seconds but he finally found what he was looking for. From here he could see a light in Miss Major's place. But at the same moment another feeling came over him. That same feeling he felt from the elevators and even his nightmare. Slowly Matthew turned in the other direction, towards the elevators.

Beyond the buildings there was still enough daylight to see the field but the mysterious circle was hidden behind Nicodemus's home. Matthew watched for a moment and had a strange feeling which was a little scary but also almost comforting. He'd never felt that before.

Nicodemus didn't know that Matthew was watching from the hotel, he couldn't even see the hotel from where he was standing right in the center of the crop circle in his field. He walked around the crop circle brushing his hand along the tall wheat stalks that still stood at the edges. Above him stars were coming out above as night fell. Nicodemus scanned the vastness of space. Then, his dog growled. Nicodemus looked around, there was no sign of anybody or anything. The growl turned to a whine as the dog pushed into Nicodemus's leg as though for safety.

"I swear you're the scared-est dog I ever saw," Nicodemus spoke softly. It was a voice that few had heard. But then something else happened that snapped Nicodemus to attention. First it was a crackling sound followed by electrical static. He looked towards the elevator where power lines began to buzz and impulses of static electricity sparked off the lines. Then several lines of static arced from the wires to the top of the elevator.

Nicodemus stared at the arcs, something was familiar about the way they danced around the wires. "I've seen this, Dog," Nicodemus said and again his voice was soft but careful, "I've seen this before."

17

Snow greeted the group as they sat quietly. Not regular snow though, it was white specks that filled the picture tube of the new television set in Bernstein's lobby.

"The picture isn't very good," said Jessup. Jessup was always the first one to complain about something so it came as no surprise to Mr. Bernstein who patiently smiled. He also ran a business, it was the drug store where people went for medicine. It was also where Matthew found the latest comic books on Wednesday afternoons.

Mr. Jessup was mostly okay but prided himself on having the best car or the best suits or the best anything.

Mr. Bernstein looked at the others for their reaction to the picture on his new set. Mrs. Bernstein rolled her eyes at him in their secret looks, the kind that married couples share between each other that nobody notices. Miss Evans, in her 60's, sat up firmly and sharp-eyed.

She was a spinster, a woman who never married. In fact nobody ever saw her with a man. But that wasn't hard to believe as most men over the age of twenty-five were married. So she lived alone in a house off Main Street and attended church and even went to the movies. Matthew knew this because he had seen her almost every time he had gone to the movies and he went all the time. Someone had said her bathroom was papered in movie star photos.

"It's an RCA Victor," Mr. Bernstein said quietly. He knew he would get a response from someone. Almost immediately the snow cleared a little and the picture became better. It was a TV western.

"It's almost as clear as my brother-in-law's set," Miss Evans said matter-of-factly, "He's got a Motorola."

Matthew and Bernie were oblivious to any comments as they were lost in the magic of the images being flashed in front of them in spite of the poor quality.

"It's just a little snowy," said the Reverend. His full name was Reverend Andrew Bates and he was a deeply religious man who preached against sin and evil in the white clapboard church at the end of Main Street. Matthew once went there with a friend when he was younger but he never really liked it that much. It had very plain walls unlike the church he attended. His church, just outside of town and beside the cemetery, had gold-colored icons and murals painted on the ceiling in bold colors. Since it was an Eastern European church and they held their services in the language of the old country. And she took Matthew every Sunday along with Babka who prayed practically during the whole service.

"Maybe the antenna needs an adjustment," added Jessup.

Bernstein shrugged, "I'll do it tomorrow."

"That should fix it," Miss Evans chimed in, "My brother-in-law had a little trouble at first too."

Matthew and Bernie hardly even heard them. Their eyes were still fixed on the moving images on the 21-inch television set. They were now part of the privileged few in Empire who had access to a TV. And right now a whole new world had opened to them. Matthew didn't have to sneak into Simpson's store anymore and risk being kicked out. He could come to the hotel lobby anytime he felt like it. Both boys leaned back to watch the show. The fact that it was a western was a bonus but they didn't care what it was as long as they could sit and watch.

But the viewing was suddenly interrupted as the lobby door swung open with a jarring crash. All eyes turned as Nicodemus entered as suddenly as the door opened. He stood there for a moment as his eyes scanned the room searching for something, or someone. Nobody spoke in that moment, everyone knew Nicodemus but yet the suddenness of his appearance left them unsure what he was doing and what he wanted. Mr. Bernstein, always being calm and soft-spoken, smiled at Nicodemus. After he scanned the lobby, his eyes laid on Mr. Bernstein.

I need to find Simpson," Nicodemus said urgently, "I need supplies. He's not at his store or house."

The Reverend felt a need to handle this unexpected guest and he chose his temperament as he looked up at Nicodemus. "Really, Mr. Johnson," he said almost condescending, "we're watching television."

Nicodemus had a strange look like he didn't quite understand. He turned slowly to look at the television and stared at it momentarily. Nothing registered to him.

"He's not here, Mr. Johnson," Mr. Bernstein said, "He might have gone to Corman, he has a sister there. What's the problem?"

Nicodemus turned to Mr. Bernstein, ignoring the Reverend. "You don't understand," he said again, emphasizing his continuing urgency. "I need supplies. There's no time to waste."

"Surely it can wait until tomorrow," Mr. Bernstein answered. And then he made a gracious sweep of his hand towards an empty chair. "Sit down, watch our television."

"There's no time," Nicodemus snapped back. Nicodemus's eyes finally fell on Matthew and Bernie and he seemed to be surprised that he hadn't noticed them sooner. His mood changed noticeably as his shoulders relaxed slightly. But his eyes continued darting back to the adults nervously.

Matthew felt awkward with Nicodemus's odd behavior. It was uncomfortable. Not quite scary but yet intense enough for everyone in the room including Matthew to feel uneasy. They sat quietly, looking at him. Matthew wondered what would happen next.

Jessup took his turn as he looked at Nicodemus. "What about them crop circles out there, Nicodemus," he said, "you make 'em?"

Nicodemus dismissed Jessup with a quick look. But he was slowly beginning to realize he was creating a spectacle of himself. It was Matthew's look that seemed to affect him the most. He could almost sense the apprehension that the boy felt.

And that brought him to the thought that nobody here was able to help him in his secret quest. He bent his head slightly, searching now for the words that would remove him from this situation that he created.

"I... I apologize," Nicodemus started, "It's just that I need to find Mr. Simpson," he stumbled, "I apologize for intruding upon all of you."

Nicodemus turned back to the door which he entered and gave Matthew a quick nod, an acknowledgment, before he walked out. When he was gone nobody spoke. Only the sound of the TV could be heard, a commercial for a dish soap.

Miss Evans was the first to speak, "It's terrible, that man should be ashamed to behave like that," she said curtly.

"He's a little confused, Miss Evans," Mr. Bernstein said, "It happens."

"What about them other flying saucer sightings been goin' on all around the country?" Jessup said matter-of-factly. Everyone turned to him as he continued, "Saw it in the paper yesterday. Front page. They don't print lies in the paper."

The Reverend was quick to answer, "If God had made beings on other planets, he would have revealed it to us in the Bible," he said solemnly, "And last time I looked, there was nothing in it about spacemen." He took a moment to assess his words, trusting that they were appropriate. But he wasn't through yet. "He's an odd man no matter what you think. Says he was in the war. He just shows up, says he lived on Thunder Hill, but nobody's there, not anymore. He's not one of us either, I never see him in church."

Miss Evans nodded and Jessup looked unsure.

Mr. Bernstein, always trying to balance things, spoke quietly again, "God is many things to many people. Mr. Johnson is a lonely man. Maybe he needs our understanding."

Matthew seemed to like what Bernie's father said, he always liked how Mr. Bernstein tried to make sure that nobody was excluded.

"Coulda been the war," Jessup spoke again, "I know some others who were never the same after combat."

The group relaxed a little, the mood was beginning to become pleasant again.

Mr. Bernstein sensed it as he looked back at the TV.

"Please, let's watch some more television. Phil Silvers is coming after this," he said. All eyes turned back to the TV.

But Matthew glanced at least two times at the door where Nicodemus had left. He wondered what was so urgent that Nicodemus would burst in and ask for Mr. Simpson in such an awkward way.

Outside, on the street, Nicodemus stood at the window of Simpson's store, looking inside. If he wasn't an adult he looked almost like a young boy gazing through the window of a toy store making a list of all the toys he would like for Christmas.

But the look on Nicodemus was less wishful and more intense as he focused on articles that he wanted urgently. Finally he gave up and turned and walked towards the ever-present elevators at the far end of Main Street. Whatever his mission was it would have to wait until tomorrow.

18

Next morning Nicodemus was all but forgotten as another day of school had begun. In class, Stephanie was passing around small square envelopes to each student, laying them on their respective desks and accompanied by a smile. She finished at Matthew's desk and took a little more time to leave as she looked into his eyes. Finally, and to Matthew's happiness, she went back to her desk and sat down, looking up towards Miss Major.

Matthew reluctantly opened the envelope. It was an invitation to her Halloween party on October 31st from two to four pm. Written on his invitation - "Looking forward to your presence," Love, Stephanie," with a few X's and O's for hugs and kisses added for good measure. Matthew was sure nobody else got the hugs and kisses and he quickly covered his invitation least someone see them.

It would be almost impossible to live that down if any of the boys caught a glimpse.

Things like that followed a kid around forever, he figured.

Once the class was settled, Miss Major stepped forward. "Now that you've all the opportunity to read your notes, I want to say that I think it's a lovely and considerate invitation on the part of Stephanie and her mother, and I've received permission from the principal for all of us to attend during the last school hour."

Now this was clearly the best thing about the party, at least to most of the class. Any opportunity to avoid school was like a bonus day. Even if it were only one hour. But it wouldn't be that easy as they would soon find out.

"Thank you for very much for the invitation, Stephanie," Miss Major added, "And I'm pleased to be included in your affair." Then she turned to the class and continued, "Class, please show your appreciation." In their usual broken unison once again, the entire class chimed in with something that sort of sounded like "Thank you, Stephanie".

Stephanie's eyes sparkled. This was her first big party beyond just a birthday party and she had planned it weeks in advance with her mother. It would be just perfect and of course it might be an excellent opportunity for Matthew to show how much he really liked her. She never really believed his dismissal of her, it was just his way of concealing his feelings. After all she was convinced that fate had a plan for both of them and they would live happily ever after, just like in the movies.

"We'll be having finger sandwiches and Freshie and chocolate cake, Miss Major," Stephanie said, "My mom and I are making everything."

Paul, always goofing off, put his hand in his mouth to gag. It got a few laughs from some of the boys but Stephanie narrowed her eyes towards him and he backed off.

"We're all looking forward to it," Miss Major said, "And I've got a special little project for the class that I think you'll enjoy."

This elicited an instant groan from the class, this was supposed to be a party and surely Miss Major wouldn't be giving them assignments. That wasn't fair or at least it shouldn't be. But teachers were always teachers. Miss Major walked slowly across the room, thinking as she moved. "I'm sure all of you remember Matthew's current event a few days ago. Well, it seems everyone's got an idea about this Emperor of Mars thing. So I thought..."

Matthew caught her words instantly and looked around the class. Some of the others were already looking at him as though anything that might happen after this was his fault.

"That each of you can show us what you think the Emperor of Mars looks like. You can draw a picture of him."

It wasn't what they expected, not really an assignment but still, they weren't exactly sure. This could take a few minutes or it could take a whole evening to do. Some of the more creative kids buzzed with excitement while some of the less creative reacted with uncertainty. Matthew wasn't entirely sure what to make of this. It sounded okay and it meant that he was off the hook with his telling the class about the Emperor.

But drawing a picture? Somehow that didn't sit well with him even if Miss Major had requested it.

Gloria was the first to raise her hand. Miss Major nodded and said, "Gloria?"

"Miss Major, exactly how should he look?"

"Use your imagination. That's what this is about, we'll all see what our imaginations can come up with."

"How about if they look like Gloria?" Paul whispered loud enough to be heard. The boys laughed as Gloria whipped around to glare at Paul with a look of pure ice that meant certain death after school.

"All right, that's enough," Miss Major interrupted. "The best drawing will appear in the weekly newspaper, along with a five dollar prize."

The stakes had suddenly risen. Now it was a competition. Five dollars was a lot of money, most allowances were around twenty-five cents. For five dollars you could buy almost anything. At least anything that a kid could want.

Matthew remained silent throughout. He had a continuing uncertainty about the whole event. It seemed to be more of a joke than the real thing. And that the crop circle was real as real gets. And then there was Nicodemus. What would he think about this?

Miss Major turned to Matthew, "Matthew. We're expecting something really special from you after all it's your story."

He tried to smile but it came off as not very convincing. For a second Miss Major's face showed some uncertainty as well, reacting to Matthew.

She recovered with her teacher smile but Matthew felt it as she walked back to her desk, she glanced back at him for just a second.

After school, Matthew and Bernie walked down Main Street. The party was still fresh in their minds.

"Boy, everybody's talking about that guy from Mars now," Bernie said, "Wonder if he's gonna bring kids?"

"It's not funny, Bernie."

"Why not? He's sorta like relatives from out of town. Just further away."

Matthew wasn't laughing. "Bernie, he's coming to tell us secrets of the universe."

"Yeah, like what?"

"Like what happens to us."

"What's that supposed't mean?"

Matthew waited, then unexpectedly, the words came out, "Like after we die."

That stopped Bernie in his tracks. He looked at Matthew who wasn't sure where the words came from. And he wasn't sure how to react. "You think some dumb spacemen who isn't even real, is gonna tell you about dying?"

"He is real. Nicodemus knows something about it too. It's got to do with the circles in his field."

"You're as dopey as Nicodemus."

The tension began to rise, both boys stepped away from each other. A line had been crossed.

"Am not!" Matthew shot back.

"Are too." Bernie answered.

Matthew looked Bernie in the eye, "He's not dumb. He's a soldier and he was in the war, and he's my friend."

Bernie waited, and then readied an answer he'd had for a long time, "You know what they say, he came back from fighting the war and that made him kinda dopey. Like you." The words were accompanied by Bernie's finger circling the side of his head.

Matthew's voice rose, "What do you know, you're a fatso."

That hit home. It was probably more than Matthew wanted to say but Bernie was pushing him and he had to say something bad. Bernie suddenly raised his fist and took a poke at Matthew. It brushed Matthew's face and he reacted by throwing a punch. Neither connected.

"You're a dumb hunkie." Bernie shouted. There were a few more swings that merely brushed by as they finally grabbed each other and started throwing wild punches until Matthew connected with a solid hit to Bernie's face. Bernie immediately stepped back and felt his nose where a trickle of blood had already started. "Dumb hunky, dumb hunky," Bernie said as he turned and ran away.

"I'm not a dumb hunky!" Matthew shouted.

Bernie stopped in his tracks and turned, pressing his finger against his bleeding nose, "You're just trying to make Nicodemus your dad because your dad never came back."

Matthew was at a loss for words, he didn't know what to say. He was just mad. Yet the words seemed to hit home harder than he'd expected. Bernie, realizing he'd gone too far, figured the best thing was to leave. He ran down the street and around a corner.

"I'm not making anybody my dad!" Matthew shouted. Matthew's whole body was shaking now and his mind was spinning with lots of different thoughts. Finally he could feel his feet moving and he realized he was walking. But it was that kind of walk that you don't notice when you're really upset, he didn't know where he was going and he didn't really care.

And that's when he saw Nicodemus's truck, parked in front of Simpson's store.

19

Matthew ran to Simpson's store and stopped in front to catch his breath. Through the window he saw Simpson talking to Nicodemus at the counter. He made a silent decision and walked inside.

Matthew entered just as Simpson handed over a long roll of electrical wiring. A few of the store regulars including Lorne and Anderson watched quietly as the transaction continued. Nobody noticed Matthew as he stood in an aisle, almost concealed from the adults. From there, he could see everything that was going on.

"Repairing the elevators?" Simpson said with a grunt.

Nicodemus didn't answer as he counted out his money, dollar bills and finally coins, until he had the right amount. Simpson glanced down at the money then at Nicodemus.

"I said, you rewiring something?"

Nicodemus pushed the money to Simpson. Simpson narrowed his eyes in that way he did when he wanted someone to know he meant business.

Matthew had seen that look more than once and he knew it was not good.

"Somethin' to do with that crop circle, maybe?"

Nicodemus plainly ignored the questions and ran his fingers across the wiring to make sure it was new.

"We got electrical code restrictions here, you just make sure you don't violate them, understand?"

Nicodemus lifted the wiring and left, passing by Matthew on the way out. He gave a sideways glance at him before he walked out the door. Matthew didn't know how to react and he lowered his eyes.

"Hey, kid."

Matthew knew the voice, it was Mr. Simpson. He'd been discovered now and anything could happen. Matthew slowly stepped out from the aisle revealing himself.

"What's your friend there up to?" Simpson asked.

Matthew thought that over. It was also the way he said it, like being Nicodemus's friend meant something less than being anyone else's friend.

"Don't know," was all that came from Matthew.

"You don't, huh," Simpson shook his head, "Well you tell him I'm keeping my eye on him."

Matthew nodded nervously and then slowly turned and walked out.

Outside, Matthew was in time to see Nicodemus drive off towards the elevators. He started walking then broke into a run as he headed towards the elevators, whose towers loomed at the end of Main Street.

By the time Nicodemus had dropped off his load of electrical wiring near the crop circle Matthew was nearly there. Nicodemus looked up to see the boy arriving, out of breath. This time Matthew sat down near the edge of the field in plain view. As he caught his breath he continued to watch Nicodemus.

Nicodemus turned back to the field and lifted a scythe with a long curved blade. Then he began to swing the blade cutting down the waist-high wheat in a path that was aimed from the circle to the grain elevators. Now and then Nicodemus would look up to see Matthew still watching. It was clear now that Nicodemus was cutting a path that when he was finished would be almost like a road leading from the crop circle to the elevators. Matthew sat there for at least two hours until finally Nicodemus stopped. He looked up at the sky where the sun was already low.

"You'd best get home, boy," Nicodemus shouted, "Get your supper."

Matthew looked up at the sky. Any moment now, his mother would be at the door of their house and calling for him. He took another look at Nicodemus and then reluctantly stood up and walked away. Nicodemus watched until Matthew was gone. Then he bent down to continue cutting the path.

At home, Matthew finished his supper of potato dumplings and watched Elana and Babka, he was waiting for the right moment.

"Nicodemus is building something on his field," he said casually.

Elana spoke without looking up, "Whatever it is, it's his business," she said quietly.

"Do you remember the ghost town on Thunder Hill," Matthew said, "Did you ever see it?"

Elana looked at him for a moment. A long-forgotten memory passed through her. It was of a better time. "I was there once with your father, Elana said slowly. "It was when we were both young, I think I was sixteen. He wanted to explore it, I was scared but he wasn't," she paused for a moment, then, "There wasn't much there, a few homes, an automobile garage and a general store. The people kept to themselves."

Matthew leaned forward, wanting to know more. She said she was sixteen. It was hard for Matthew to imagine his mother as being the same age as the high school teens he saw at school. He had seen them smoking and even saw a boy and girl kissing once. He wondered if she had done any of those things and also thought about what she was like before she was a mother and a widow.

"Everyone says the town came out of the ground," Matthew pressed, "And that the people who lived there were spirits and when it was time, they went back under the earth and now they just wait."

Elana shrugged, "The people left, that's all."

"He doesn't have any family or anything," Matthew continued, "I think sometimes he just wants someone to talk to."

"Mr. Johnson had a hard life, I think," she answered, and then added, "Not like your movie shows. Not everyone has a good life."

"In school they tell us we can become anything," Matthew suddenly spurted out. He wasn't even sure why he had said that so suddenly, but then he added, "Doctors and policemen and lawyers and even famous actors."

"That's not for ordinary people," was Elana's answer as she finished her supper.

"Why are we ordinary? Was dad ordinary? Why did he go to war?"

Elana glanced at Babka, who sat quietly eating. Then she looked at Matthew, "He said it was the right thing."

"What was he like?"

Elana took a long moment to study Matthew, then, "He was like you, he liked the movie shows. Once he took me, but it was foolishness, people pretending to be other people. I didn't like the movies." But then another memory came back to her for a few seconds she drifted back to another time and place. "He liked them though. That's why I took you to one when you were too young."

Matthew was almost sorry he had asked the question when he watched her turn and get up and carry the dishes to the kitchen sink. It was always like this when talk of his father came up and Matthew guessed that she probably missed him a lot. He just wasn't sure what it was that was to be missed.

Elana went to the cupboard and pulled out a small cake covered with wax paper. She cut a piece for Matthew and brought it over to him. Matthew looked away from her because he didn't like it when she was sad. He was sorry he brought up his father. Then he looked at the clock. Matthew grabbed the piece of cake and ran outside. Elana glanced after him, still lost in her own memory of her husband.

Nicodemus, coffee in hand, walked slowly to the door of his house, wondering who had just knocked. He opened it cautiously to reveal Matthew standing in the warm light filtering out into the darkness. His bike lay on the ground.

Matthew stood there holding the cake wrapped in his handkerchief.

"I brought you some cake," Matthew said.

It took Nicodemus by surprise and for a moment, he wasn't sure what to do next.

"I don't want any," he answered.

"It's good, my mom made it, it was for me, I thought you'd want some," Matthew countered.

Nicodemus stood back, shaking his head, "Why do you bother me, boy? I got work to do."

Matthew still held the cake towards Nicodemus. Then he said, "Because I believe you. I want to see him as much as you do."

Nicodemus stared at the boy for a long moment, as though deciding on something Finally he spoke.

"Who?"

Matthew took a deep breath, "The Emperor of Mars."

Nicodemus looked at the boy and realized he was not leaving. He looked at the cake again, "Cake, huh?"

There was enough cake for both of them as Nicodemus studied Matthew for a moment, then he walked into his house and came back with a second cup of coffee. He handed it to Matthew. They sat outside and ate the cake in silence. No words passed between them, just a look now and then. Finally, Matthew spoke.

"You know, the way you're going you're not gonna have much of a field left."

"Nobody's gonna miss that little bit of wheat," Nicodemus answered as he looked up at a clock, "It's late, you go home now."

"I can stay."

"It's dark, your mother will be worried. Go home."

Matthew knew he was right. It was dark outside and he should be at home.

"I'll be back tomorrow," Matthew said, watching for any reaction from Nicodemus.

"Tomorrow then," was all he said.

Near them the tall elevators were dark and ominous as Matthew climbed on his bike. He turned to Nicodemus silhouetted in the light coming from his kitchen.

"There's more cake," Matthew said, "I can bring more."

Nicodemus didn't answer, instead he turned and closed the door behind him. In the darkness, Matthew began to peddle past the elevators.

Once he was gone, Nicodemus stepped outside and looked towards the field where a few blue sparks rose from the part of the field he had cut down. He didn't know what it was but the look on his face suggested that it would change everything around here once it was known exactly why it was happening.

And things wouldn't be the same in Empire again.

20

Matthew made a detour on the way home. He deliberately decided to pass by the movie theater. He knew what was showing that night, an adult-rated film. Adult meant that he couldn't see it. While he wasn't sure why, it was usually because the story was about something kids weren't supposed to see.

Once he had sneaked into an adult film and found it very boring. All people did was talk and talk and look upset and cry.

Frankly Matthew didn't see what the fuss was all about. Now as he stood in front of the window looking in, he considered sneaking in again just to see if this movie was better. The poster boldly illustrated a woman with very little clothing.

But just as his hand reached for the door Mr. Kiminsky appeared to clean up the popcorn machine. Matthew stepped back into the shadows. He knew that Mr. Kiminsky wouldn't let him see an adult film and that he should be going home, that Elana would be worried. But he just needed to know what the movie was about. Then he did what he had done before and walked around the corner taking his bike with him. If he couldn't see the movie then he could hear it.

Matthew came around the back of the theater and leaned his bike against the fire exit door. Nobody every came out this way, in fact, Matthew wasn't even sure if it even opened. He held his breath as he listened. The sound of the movie, mostly people talking, slowly came to him as he listened carefully. After a moment, Matthew sat down on the tiny door ledge and leaned his head back listening to the words being spoken on the screen on the other side of the door. He began to imagine the actors, playing out the story for him. They moved around him acting their roles in the dark, dusty alley behind the theater and Matthew closed his eyes.

When Matthew opened his eyes again, the movie was over. He suddenly remembered where he was and that he was supposed to be home and in bed. Matthew got up and walked his bike to the sidewalk as the last few movie patrons left. Then he saw her.

Miss Major.

Miss Major didn't see Matthew as she walked out of the theater and down the sidewalk to Main Street. He had slipped back into the shadows where he was hidden from the light. Matthew waited until everyone was gone then he stepped out onto the sidewalk. There was nobody in sight.

Matthew knew that he should go home but something was running through his mind. Miss Major had left the theater alone but he was curious where she would go. He felt like one of those spies in the spy movies watching somebody who didn't know they were being watched. Matthew wondered if that was wrong. But he wasn't doing anything bad, not like Tommy, who the kids said watched people through their windows at night. Matthew wasn't like Tommy at all. He just wanted to see where Miss Major was going.

Matthew turned his bike onto Main Street and stopped. There were a few trucks and a car parked by the Crescent Café and the neon sign was still on. Sam usually kept his café open after the movie let out as some of the moviegoers would drop by for a coffee or a hamburger. Matthew looked down Main Street and there was no sign of Miss Major so he decided to go to the cafe.

When he reached the café, he no sooner parked his bike when he glanced into the window and saw Miss Major. She was getting a cup of coffee from Sam. That seemed harmless enough to Matthew. But then she looked across the café and Matthew followed her look right to a booth against the other wall.

Nicodemus sat there alone with a coffee.

Miss Major wasn't sure exactly why she chose to walk up to Nicodemus or at least she didn't think she did. She wanted to think it was about Matthew and her concern for him and the Emperor of Mars thing but she knew it was more than that. She felt drawn to Nicodemus, maybe it was the loneliness that seemed to flow from him, maybe it was her own loneliness at being so far away from her home and family and friends. Maybe it was something else.

"Mr. Johnson," she said nervously.

Nicodemus looked up. She found herself stumbling for words.

"I... I'm Miss Major, I'm Matthew's teacher," she managed to continue, "I was wondering if I could talk to you for a minute."

Nicodemus studied her, unsure of what this woman wanted. Some deep part of him thought that she could be an angel if this wasn't Empire. He didn't even know where that thought came from as she stood there waiting. He nodded for her to sit across from him.

It was a big decision for her as well yet something told her she wanted to know more about this man. She sat down.

Outside Matthew could not believe his eyes. Of all the surprises he'd witnessed in the last few days this one topped them all. Miss Major was sitting with Nicodemus. The only two people with whom he had something to do with were sitting together. Without him. And he didn't like it at all.

"Matthew says he's been at your place," Miss Major said. "He's got this silly idea about the Emperor of Mars and..."

"Why are you asking me about the boy?" Nicodemus interrupted.

I... uh, well, he seems to be strongly influenced by you," she managed to say, "His father was killed in the war."

Nicodemus stared away, "A lot of men were killed in the war," he answered.

There was a moment of silence. Miss Major wasn't sure what to say next but somehow the words came out. "Nobody seems to agree on you, Mr. Johnson. Some say you lived in that town on Thunder Hill, others say you never lived anywhere around here."

"Most people don't know much about you, either."

His instant reaction to her words set her aback again. He was right, of course but it was plain and clear that Nicodemus Johnson had no time for idle talk.

"I'm from Durham, eighty miles south," she said, surprising herself again, "I guess we're both strangers here. Maybe that's why I came over. Even small towns can be hard to get into, at first."

Outside, Matthew continued to watch, getting more uncomfortable the longer Miss Major and Nicodemus sat there, looking at each other. He couldn't hear what they said but imagined it could be just about anything. He hoped it was about him. What was more disturbing was Miss Major's behavior. She seemed different somehow. She wasn't his teacher right now but something else. She sat and moved in a different way than in school and even when he saw her at her apartment. Even the way she leaned her head forward was different.

Then it came to him, she was acting like a grown woman. It was a funny thought, of course she was a woman, but not like his mom or other moms. She was still young.

"Can I ask you something?" Miss Major said to Nicodemus as he sipped coffee. He shrugged, still unsure what this angel of a woman wanted.

"What?"

When the war was over, did you make it to Paris, I mean, did you see it?"

Nicodemus realized he was staring at her and slowly turned his gaze away to something else as a memory flashed back to him. It was a memory of the lights of the Eiffel Tower glistening on a Parisian night.

"I saw Paris towards the end."

"What was it like?"

Another image floated through his mind, walking along the Seine River with French people celebrating.

"People on the streets, at cafes, people walking along the river. Big churches."

"Not like here, I guess," Miss Major said.

The memories floated away from Nicodemus as he looked at her.

"Home is home."

"But it must have been beautiful," she said.

"It was," he said unexpectedly. "Like nowhere else on earth."

Outside, Matthew felt himself becoming sad. There was something wrong with this, him watching Miss Major and Nicodemus. He wasn't sure if it was anger or hurt. Right now he needed to go away. He didn't want to see them anymore. Matthew climbed on his bike and rode off down Main Street.

Neither Nicodemus nor Miss Major had seen Matthew. They were sitting there now not saying much more. Finally Nicodemus put down his empty coffee cup. There was an awkward moment when he felt a need to stay. But he quickly put that thought away.

"I have to go," was all he said as he stood up.

"Maybe we can... maybe have a coffee again sometime?" she surprised herself, "Two strangers?"

There was something so graceful and so non-threatening about her question that Nicodemus even surprised himself when he spoke.

"That would be okay."

And with that, he turned and left before he might say something else, something that would ruin this moment with the angel. Miss Major watched him walk out the door. She stared for what seemed like a long time until she realized Sam was watching her. He smiled and asked if she wanted more coffee.

Matthew watched from behind a wall as Nicodemus walked away. Then he rode as hard as he could to get away from the café. It was like that time with Bernie where he was so angry he didn't know where he was even going. He finally stopped and climbed off his bike and caught his breath. It took a minute or two but he realized he was near the railroad tracks and the elevators. Somehow he had ridden this way rather than going home.

Home. His mother was never going to let him out at night anymore after this. He climbed back on the bike to start riding when a strange sound made him turn. It was coming from an elevator. It was low and almost a hum. Matthew thought it could have been a cat or maybe dog but it sounded oddly human.

"Anybody there?" he said loudly.

The low hum now sounded more like a groan. And it wasn't an animal. Then he heard a swooshing sound behind him and Matthew turned to see a silver shape the size of a man float right past him. But before he could ride away something behind him grabbed his bike. Matthew turned again to see two silver figures standing before him with arms waving, moving closer towards him.

21

Something strange began to rumble in Matthew's heart as he trembled with fear. Something deep within him that told him not to run. He really didn't understand it but it was a feeling that ran stronger than his fear. He realized that maybe, just maybe, this was what he was waiting for.

Matthew straightened up, took a deep breath and stared at the two shining figures in front of him.

"Hello," he said apprehensively.

They didn't answer.

"I'm Matthew," he stammered, "uh, welcome to Earth... uh, sir..."

The silver figures swept past him knocking him down as they danced around. Then one of them spoke in an odd tin-like voice.

"Where's my money, Earth child?"

There was something vaguely familiar about the voice as Matthew climbed to his feet and stood up.

"Give me my money or you will be blasted into space!"

The speaking figure aimed his hand at Matthew as sparks shot out and fell to the ground. Matthew knew what it was, a five cent sparkler and it was becoming evident to him that this was not the Emperor. As the sparks sizzled out Matthew now knew the identity of the two figures.

"Tommy," he said.

Tommy, his face leaning out of the aluminum foil he'd bent and shaped around his body, laughed out loud. His friend Elvin, now revealed and also wrapped in foil, grabbed Matthew and lifted him off the ground holding him tightly.

"Earth child, give us money!" said Elvin.

Matthew struggled to get out of Elvin's grip, pulling off some of the older boy's tin foil.

"Let me go!" Matthew shouted. Not only was Elvin hurting him it was also horribly embarrassing to be lifted up like that with his feet kicking.

"What are you gonna do, baby?" Tommy said, "Cry?"

Matthew suddenly was filled with anger and even though Elvin was holding him, Matthew swung his fist as hard as he could.

The punch caught Tommy by surprise and connected just under his chin. It was enough of a blow to knock him off balance. Suddenly all was silent. Tommy felt his chin where a red bruise was forming. Elvin dropped Matthew and just stood there.

At the same instant Matthew realized he was dead for sure. But try as he did, he simply could not make his feet move forward.

He was frozen on the spot like in a bad dream. Just as Tommy started towards Matthew with his fists raised, a tall dark figure stepped between them.

"What's going on here?"

Tommy and Elvin turned slowly to see Nicodemus standing in their way. Without hesitation the two bullies decided to beat it and they ran off into the dark. Nicodemus leaned down to Matthew.

"Are you okay?" he asked in a calm voice.

Matthew turned away for a moment and wiped away a single tear that he felt on his cheek. He didn't want Nicodemus or anyone else for that matter see him cry.

"Yeah," was all he could manage.

"I swear you and that Tommy seem to be mortal enemies," said Nicodemus almost light-heartedly. He'd noticed Matthew wipe away the tear. "It's okay. Tears are okay." He continued, "I've seen brave soldiers cry where I was." Matthew nodded as he wiped the last tear away.

"You probably could use some coffee," Nicodemus added.

Inside Nicodemus's house was simpler than Matthew expected. As Nicodemus was getting coffee Matthew looked around the room. It had a table, two chairs and a wood stove. There was a recycled trunk and a rocking chair and a desk in the corner that kept the elevator bookkeeping. And there was a bookcase that held several worn books, some with library tags on them. Matthew caught the names of a few, *1984*, *War of the Worlds* and a book on stars and constellations.

There were two photographs on the trunk that drew Matthew to them. One had a younger Nicodemus with several men all in military uniforms. Another was of a beautiful young woman standing in front of a cafe called Thunder Hill Café.

"Watch it, it's hot," Nicodemus said as he came over with two cups of coffee.

Matthew gripped the tin cup lightly as the steam rose from its rim. Matthew looked away for a second as he relived the previous ordeal. "I really thought they were real spacemen. I can't believe it, I fell for it, just like a Grade One. Everybody's gonna know tomorrow."

"Worse things can happen to a man than getting laughed at," Nicodemus said with a sad look.

There was something about those words that seemed to suggest a greater hurt within him. He noticed Matthew looking at the photographs. "Me on the left there," he pointed, "Andy and Homer and Jack are the others."

By now Matthew was transfixed by the beautiful woman in the photo. Nicodemus's expression changed slightly with a hint of a smile.

"Who's she?" Matthew asked.

"That's my Mary," Nicodemus replied.

"Is she dead?" Matthew asked quietly.

Nicodemus looked at Matthew and shook his head, "You don't waste much time, do you, boy?"

"Whattya mean?"

"Some things, you should work up to, don't just ask them outright."

"Why not?"

"Because you don't."

Matthew thought about it for a moment. Then he turned to Nicodemus. "My dad died, everyone in town knows that. I don't mind."

Nicodemus moved away from the photographs and sat in the rocker gripping his tin cup of coffee. He took a sip. Matthew watched and took a sip of his coffee. It was black and hot and bitter to his taste. Yet he felt he must grow to like it.

"Do you pray alot?" he asked.

"Boy, you ask a lot of questions."

Matthew shrugged, his mother said he asked a lot of questions and he wondered what was wrong with that. After all he was only twelve years old and there were a lot of things to learn yet. "My name's Matthew, not boy," he said. "Just asked because my grandmother prays all the time, Mom says the older you are the more people you got to pray for." He paused for a second, and then continued. "So?"

"So what?"

"Do you pray alot?"

Nicodemus took a moment to reflect on that answer. It was much more complicated than the boy could possibly understand at his tender age. "Praying's for those who choose to believe praying helps," Nicodemus answered. "Some folks figure other things help."

"Like what?"

Nicodemus shook his head yet again. "Don't you learn anything at school?"

"Not about praying."

"Boy, drink your coffee."

Matthew realized the quiz was over. Nicodemus sipped his coffee and stared at the old photographs.

Matthew sipped more of the hot bitter coffee. And he remembered that he should have been home long ago. He gulped down the rest of his coffee and stood up.

"I gotta get home otherwise I'll be in big trouble. It's been a long night."

Nicodemus smiled, "Guess it has," He paused and then added, "Matthew." Matthew liked that.

Outside Nicodemus's house Matthew climbed on his bike and turned to the house where Nicodemus stood in the light. For a moment he almost seemed to sparkle himself and Matthew had to look twice to make sure. The second time the sparkle was gone. But it sure did seem like it was there the first time.

"See ya later, Mr. Johnson," Matthew said. Then he thought of something else to say and decided to say it quickly. "Maybe next time I can help you with the construction."

Nicodemus seemed to be considering it. "You ask your momma first," he said almost reluctantly. Then he added, "An' if you're gonna hang around, you call me Nicodemus. Mr. Johnson makes me feel old."

Matthew pushed off and rode his bike away. "And stay away from that Simpson boy," Nicodemus added. He stood watching till he couldn't see the boy any more. Then he looked up at the elevators and his smile turned to a frown.

From high up on the elevator, the wind stirred and it felt like a presence of some kind had appeared and was looking down at Nicodemus as he turned in the doorway and went inside. The warm light from the house disappeared as the door closed.

But up at the top of the elevator, the wood structure creaked and groaned as though it were in the most terrible pain. And only the dog heard it and he whimpered as though he was afraid.

22

What remained of the ghostly space creatures hung from a tree near the school the next morning. That way everyone who walked or ran past it on their way to school would see it. And they would know. Word would spread among the students like fire in a small town like Empire about the great deception and how Matthew fell for it.

And just to make sure a hand-written sign was pinned to its chest in bold letters. Matthew's Martian.

Matthew walked slowly past the hanging foil and pulled the sign off and crumbled it into the palm of his hand.

But the damage was done. Not far away a few of the Grade 8's were watching him and whispering. He held his head high and walked into the schoolyard as though nothing happened. Then Bernie appeared.

"Tommy told everybody," he said with a shrug, "Did you really think it was spacemen?"

Matthew walked past him. Bernie ran to catch up.

"Well, didya?"

Matthew spoke without looking at him.

"I got work to do."

He opened the door to the classrooms and walked in, letting the door close in front of Bernie.

Even though Matthew walked softly into the classroom, Miss Major sensed he was there. She, like the other teachers, had already heard about the embarrassing incident and she knew she had to be sensitive enough to make him feel like everything was okay. For now she would talk like nothing happened.

"Good morning, Matthew."

He looked at her for a second and then turned towards the blackboards. Her behavior last night with Nicodemus had not been forgotten or forgiven. For Matthew last night was a double disaster. "Good morning," he mumbled as he began taking the brushes and chalk out.

"Matthew," Miss Major said quietly.

She came up to him, holding a book up. "I thought you might like to read this," she said, lifting it for him to see. "It's not as boring as it looks. There's lots of pictures."

Matthew looked at the book. It was an art book about French impressionist painters. The painting on the cover was very much like the one Miss Major and he had put up on her wall. But that was before.

"Thank you," he said coldly, and took the book. He set it down and returned to his job turning his back to her. Miss Major figured that this was about the embarrassing incident but she didn't know that she herself was responsible for at least part of his mood.

When the classroom was filled and ready to begin Miss Major decided to comment on what everyone in the room was thinking about. As the class sat, hands in position, she stepped in front of her desk.

"Before we begin our regular class, I want to talk to you about something," she said in her best teacher voice. This had to be serious and even though she was new at teaching she had practiced her serious voice many times in front of a mirror.

Matthew looked up at her, suspicious. He had a bad feeling whatever would happen next was about him.

Hadn't he had enough trouble? His mother had been furious at his coming home late and said he was not allowed to go see a movie until she decided it was okay again. That could be forever, he thought.

Stephanie watched Matthew from her desk, she felt his pain and wished there were something that she could do or say. Maybe afterward, she thought, she would bring him something to cheer him up. A gift of some kind.

"There's a mean story going around about last night" Miss Major started, "It was a very cruel joke that could have been intended for any one of us. How would you have reacted? I know I would have probably been scared out of my wits. It's not a very nice thing to do to anybody, is it?"

Matthew sank his head lower, wishing he could disappear. Why was she doing this to him, he thought. But somehow he knew she was doing it for him rather than to him. It just wasn't going to be easy.

"Think about it before you laugh at anybody else." She continued. "It could have been you or maybe an elderly person. Would you want that? Of course not. I don't want to see anybody laughing about it. Understood?"

There was no movement in the class as they sat there looking at Miss Major or stealing a glance at Matthew who looked down at his desk.

"Good" Miss Major said sharply, "Now, Matthew and Bernie."

They both looked at her.

"I want both of you to go outside and take that awful thing down from the tree and throw it in the garbage. I don't know why someone hadn't done that earlier."

Bernie got up first and looked at Matthew. He knew what his Matthew was going through and he knew they had an argument. But this was the time to stand up for your best friend regardless.

"Yes, Miss Major," Bernie said and started for the door. Matthew got up slowly and shuffled behind him. They both left the classroom under watching eyes. Once they were gone, Miss Major turned to the class again.

"Remember, class, what happened to Matthew could have happened to anyone of us."

Stephanie nodded to herself as she listened. A boy near her giggled and Stephanie turned to him with ice cold eyes that suggested he might be better off keeping his joke to himself. She made a fist and shook it. He contemplated the look and quickly shut up and turned to look at Miss Major.

Outside, Matthew and Bernie silently gathered the foil bunched it up and carried it to a trash can near the school entrance. They glanced at each other as they worked but neither spoke until Bernie finally broke the silence.

"I'm sorry about calling you a hunky," Bernie said. "And what I said about your dad."

Matthew looked at his best friend.

"I'm sorry 'bout calling you fatso."

With those few words the fight was officially over. Both boys relaxed. Things were back to normal. At least for them.

"One of these days," Bernie said, "Tommy's gonna get his. I just hope I'm there."

By the time school had let up Nicodemus had made a pretty good start on the pathway. It was about twenty feet wide and led through the wheat from the circle to the elevator. Now Nicodemus had begun building a wooden foundation in the middle of the circle.

Matthew arrived as fast as his bike could carry him from school. Today was the beginning of him helping Nicodemus. He hadn't really mentioned it to his mother but as long as he was home for supper she wouldn't really have to know.

Matthew approached Nicodemus carefully. Even though he thought they'd agreed that he'd help he never knew with someone like Nicodemus. There still was the issue of Miss

Major and him but Matthew felt that could wait until the proper time.

Nicodemus looked up to see Matthew. It took him a moment, but finally, he spoke.

"I need some of them nails over there."

Matthew looked at a pile of nails Nicodemus had gathered. Some were new, some were old and rusty. He reached down and gathered a handful of nails and carried them over to Nicodemus who motioned with his hammer to a spot on the wood.

Then he grabbed a few and began nailing them. Matthew watched silently but there were burning questions in his mind.

"Do you think he was here before?"

"Who?"

"The Emperor of Mars."

Nicodemus drove a nail into the wood.

"I don't know."

The answer was interesting, for the first time Matthew had what seemed like a confirmation that there really was an Emperor of Mars.

"Why are you building this?"

"Because I have to."

"Why?"

Nicodemus drove another nail into the wood and wiped his brow. "Some things in life have no reason they just have to be done."

Matthew remembered something, "Dolores Anderson's mother saw a flying saucer."

"She saw a rock, a meteorite. They fall all the time. Hand me those long nails."

Matthew handed him a handful of nails as he looked at the crop circle.

"Well, you don't see a circle like this all the time," Matthew said, "I think you know more than you're telling me because I'm just a kid." Just then another thought came to him and he added, ""What was up there on Thunder Hill?"

Nicodemus stopped nailing and looked down at Matthew. For a moment, Matthew thought he may have gone too far, that he had asked one question too many.

"You come to talk or you come to help," Nicodemus said.

"Help," answered Matthew.

"Then get me some of those ten-penny nails over there, the bright shiny new ones."

Matthew smiled. He was still here and that meant he was closer to the Emperor of Mars than anywhere in town. Whatever was going to happen something made him feel that Nicodemus could handle it.

By suppertime, Nicodemus had to make Matthew go home. Now he was riding along on his bike and the embarrassment of the previous night was almost gone. It still hung in there a little as did Miss Major and her seeming interest in Nicodemus. There was so much Matthew didn't understand and women were one of those things. Then he wondered what it would be like to have a father to talk to about all the things he didn't understand. But he wasn't sure what that would be like either.

There was another thought that kept running through his mind. Nicodemus didn't want to talk about Thunder Hill even though it was supposed to be his home. Matthew wondered why he wouldn't talk about it. He had pictures, Matthew had seen those. Pictures of men like him and the woman he said was his wife. Mary.

As Matthew came to an intersection of streets, he could see Thunder Hill at the far end of the street where the town ended and the wide open prairie began. There was a cloud hanging over it like a giant umbrella over a haystack. It wasn't all that far either. Once Bernie and he attempted to ride their bikes there but they never made it because it began to rain. Maybe he should try again. Now that he knew more about it from what his mother and Nicodemus said, maybe there would be some answers there. But it was easily a two hour bike ride over gravel roads and that meant missing supper.

Something else brought Matthew back to the present. It was the sound of another bike approaching.

The sound was different than Bernie's, he still had a piece of cardboard pinned to his rear wheel to give it a motorcycle sound. This bike was smooth and even.

Then something else occurred to him. Music. Music was coming from somewhere else. Crackling music.

"Hi Matthew," Stephanie said as she rode up to Matthew in her new, shiny bike. It even had pink fringes hanging from the handlebars. And there was something else on the handlebars, a red plastic box where the music was coming from. It was a transistor radio. He had seen some of the teenagers with such a radio. It didn't need to be plugged in and it barely brought in the distant radio station.

Matthew looked down the street at the distant Thunder Hill and made a choice. He began to pedal. Stephanie started after him and caught up quickly.

"I got a transistor radio," she said breathing hard, "See, it plays anywhere. I can let you use it, if you want?"

"I gotta go now, Stephanie." Matthew said as he pushed harder.

"I can ride with you," Stephanie smiled, "besides I wanna tell you I think my brother did a rotten thing to you last night."

Matthew stopped. He whirled around to confront her.

"Why don't you go home?"

"It's a free country," she snapped back. Then, almost as an afterthought, she added, "You're not being nice. Didn't your mother tell you you're supposed to be nice to girls?" She caught her breath, "Anyways, I just wanted to remind you about my party."

"I can't come," Matthew answered.

"But you have to come. It's going to be a perfect party and..."

"And what!"

"We're going to have music and we can dance."

DANCE! The very sound of the word struck terror in Matthew's heart. He was not about to dance with anybody. He never even liked it when the teenagers had a sock hop in the gym and they danced to rock and roll. No sir. Dancing was not on his agenda. Ever.

Matthew began pedaling as fast as he could, leaving Stephanie behind. She started to follow but he quickly outdistanced her and she finally gave up. Stephanie watched Matthew disappear down the street. By the time he felt he was safe from Stephanie's invitations he found himself at the edge of town. He stopped to catch his breath as the silence of the open prairie greeted him. But mostly it was quiet. Beyond the town there were farms and hills and only the wind as it brushed the wheat fields.

He looked towards Thunder Hill again. The dark cloud still hung over it but now more like a shroud. He hesitated for a moment, realizing the commitment that lay ahead. As if it was an answer a clap of thunder boomed in the distance. Matthew knew he had to see what was up there no matter of the consequences. He began to pedal towards the open prairie and the darkening sky

23

By the time Matthew reached the foot of Thunder Hill the sky had darkened noticeably. A stronger wind had risen from the west causing the wheat fields to sway harder as cloud shadows moved across them like giant masted ships passing overhead. Matthew always thought this must be what the ocean was like with waves moving back and forth. Only this was wheat fields with golden waves.

It had taken him over an hour of hard riding to reach the foot of the mountain and he needed to catch his breath for a moment. He looked back at the gravel road that led straight to Empire. From here the elevators were instantly noticeable, towering over a clump of trees that hid most of the town.

He turned to the mountain again. The gravel road turned into a dirt road that led upwards, winding its way to the top. One thing was for sure, the dark cloud still hung over the mountain and now and then came the sound of distant thunder. But that was the legend and like every kid in town, Matthew knew the stories about how it rose in the middle of the night. It was a little hard to believe and he often suspected that it was just a story. But standing here now, he began to have some apprehension. Maybe it wasn't such a good idea.

That's when Matthew heard a creaking sound nearby. He jumped a little then looked on the side of the dirt road. There was an old sign hanging onto what was left of a fence post. Matthew walked his bike to the sign and lifted it to read. Faded, peeling lettering read Thunder Hill and an arrow pointed towards the dirt road. It took Matthew another thirty minutes to reach the top of Thunder Hill. He rode his bike up for half the way but when it got too steep, he had to get off and walk the bike. Finally he abandoned it to be recovered on his way down and he ran the last hundred feet.

From the top of Thunder Hill, Matthew could see almost forever. Or at least as far as the horizon.

He could easily see the whole of Empire from this height. But he wasn't here for the view and Matthew began walking along the road which now was covered with grass and weeds. Nobody had been here for a long time.

The first building he saw was barely a wall with a door hanging on an angle. The wind had become a little stronger up here and it made the door creak with an eerie sound. Further up the street was another building that still had four walls and a roof.

Matthew walked toward it. On his way he picked out foundations where other buildings used to be. Wood frames had fallen long ago and were mostly covered with dirt or grass and weeds. As he continued he saw what looked like a house partially concealed by aspen trees. They were not tall; it was probably the elevation that kept the trees from growing taller up here. But the house was worth looking into.

As he came closer he realized that some of the trees had actually begun growing through the house and that the roof was completely gone. It was a house of four walls with mature trees inside of it. Matthew had never seen anything like that and he wondered how long it took for that to happen. He knew the war was long ago, but could that have been long enough for these trees to grow through a house? Could all the buildings have aged so quickly?

One answer came to him as he stepped up to the house. To its left and hidden among the clump of aspens sat the charred ruins of another house. Fire had destroyed it. That could explain why most of the town was gone. But had fire destroyed all of it?

Matthew reached for the door handle of the tree house and pulled. It creaked open and he stepped inside.

Inside, daylight streamed through the tree branches in dappled shapes. The place was empty, no furniture at all. Wallpaper was musty and faded from the rain and snow that must have fallen inside since the roof was gone. Pieces of the roof lay rotted on the floor. Then he saw something else. A newspaper.

Matthew delicately lifted the thick, damp yellowed newspaper up. Pages were stuck together and the lettering was faded. As he raised it, some of the rotted bottom fell away and its weight ripped apart what was left of the front page.

But Matthew held onto it softly and now could read it. It was a headline that said LOCAL BOYS OFF TO EUROPE.

There was a photograph as well with several soldiers in uniform posing. But it was faded so badly that Matthew could barely make out the faces. He recognized it as the same one Nicodemus had and he looked towards the position where Nicodemus had stood.

It was hard to tell because the photograph was so badly aged. But it looked like Nicodemus.

In that same instant a wind draft came through the open door and lifted the front page from Matthew's delicate grip and spiraled up towards the tree branches where it got stuck. It was too high for Matthew to retrieve and the almost magical action itself made him conjure up images of ghosts or other kinds of things he didn't want to see. The wind had picked up and now the aspens were shimmering as their leaves made a soft low shushing sound. So far Matthew had found nothing that would help him explain Nicodemus any more nor about the mystery as to why the town had been abandoned.

Dozens of grasshoppers leaped out of the way as Matthew made his way through tall prairie grass towards the other standing building. But by the time he reached it he realized it was nearly gone as well. The roof had caved in and there were also indications of fire damage.

Then he saw the sign. It was cracked and aged and said THUNDER HILL CAFE. It was the sign he had seen in Nicodemus's photograph.

Matthew approached the window and looked inside. There was nothing but rotted floors with weeds and grass growing from them. He leaned against the window and the whole building creaked. He stepped back quickly, realizing it could all come down.

As Matthew stepped away from the café, something else caught his eye. He turned slowly, unsure, but when he saw it, his eyes opened as wide as they could and he was speechless. There, less than twenty feet away were two circles burned into the grass just like the circle in Nicodemus's field. And Matthew knew there must be a connection.

Just then a crack of thunder made Matthew jump. He looked up at the darkening sky where a bolt of lightning blasted into the earth less than fifty feet away. Smoke drifted up from the seared earth. At the same instant a stronger wind came up blowing hard across the top of Thunder Hill. The buildings creaked and the aspens hissed.

Suddenly, Matthew heard the crash of wood and turned to see the cafe collapsing in the strong wind. It was time to leave. He ran down the road as rain began to fall and the wind increased. As he ran the wind spun dust devils that twisted after him like tiny tornados.

And by the time Matthew reached his bike the wind and rain mysteriously had stopped. He looked up towards the top of Thunder Hill and considered going back. But maybe that wasn't a good idea. He mounted his bike and road as fast as he dared down towards the bottom.

24

Matthew ate his supper with careful glances around the table, not catching Elana's look. Babka ate quietly as she always did. He knew he was in trouble again but didn't want to bring it any undue attention. Somehow he figured that if he didn't think he had done anything wrong, then somehow, some way, nobody else would. But life doesn't work like that, especially for twelve-year-old boys. It had finally caught up to him when Elana sat down.

"What were you doing last night and today? She asked without looking up from her plate. Matthew knew he had to answer her.

"I'm helping Nicodemus," he answered very casually, as though it were as normal as saying he was going to see Bernie.

"What are you doing there all the time?" This time, she looked straight at him.

"Building."

"Building what?"

"Just stuff."

"Does he pay you?"

"It's not that kind of stuff."

"What kind of "stuff" is it then?"

Matthew finished his supper and took his plate to the sink. "It's a surprise, sort of, you'll see it soon," he said as he headed for the door. It was only ten feet away and if he could make it out the door before she spoke, he was home-free. He closed his eyes and wished all his might that she'd let him go.

"Just till dark," she said instead.

Matthew never expected her to say that. He was ready for a big "no," but instead he got a "just till dark." He wanted to turn around and hug her and thank her but he thought that might arouse too much suspicion so he let it go. As he ran out the door, he shouted back.

"I'll be back before dark."

Matthew rode his bike down Main Street. As always, it was quiet. A few trucks were parked at the café and a car in front of the hotel that he'd never seen meant someone was staying in one of the rooms. As he rode past the hotel, Bernie appeared, riding his bike. They rode in silence for a moment until Bernie finally broke the quiet.

"What's Nicodemus building??

"Nothing."

"Come on, you know."

"It's secret."

"I heard someone say it's a landing pad for flying saucers," Bernie said with a glance toward Matthew.

"Maybe."

"Can I see?"

"Maybe, later."

"I can't stay out after eight on a school night."

Both boys stopped in the middle of the street. Since there was no danger of any traffic, they stood there as they talked.

"Since when?" Matthew asked.

"Since the TV," he replied, "My parents won't let me. They found a new way to punish me. No TV. Boy, just when I thought TV was a good thing too."

Matthew thought it over for a moment. Since Bernie was his best friend it seemed that he had a right to know. He wasn't sure that Nicodemus would approve but friendship is friendship and if Nicodemus said no, Matthew would have to convince him that Bernie was all right.

In the field, Nicodemus already had partially finished a platform near the elevators and right in the path he had cut days before. He was placing small firepots along one side of the path, starting at the crop circle and leading to the platform. The firepots were army surplus, small round metal containers the size of a bowling ball and set about five feet apart. They were used mostly for illuminating temporary airfields that were often just open fields.

As Nicodemus set up the last firepot, he noticed Matthew and Bernie approaching on their bikes.

"Nicodemus," Matthew said, unsure of what his reaction to Bernie would be. "This is Bernie, he's my best friend and he wants to help too, at least until seven o'clock."

Nicodemus studied Bernie for a brief moment. Bernie's excitement at what Nicodemus had done to the field was more than enthusiastic. "Whatchya doing?" he exclaimed loudly. Matthew poked him in the arm. Bernie got the message and toned down a little.

Nicodemus hid a smile as he watched the two boys. Somehow, it brought back a memory to him, of a childhood long, long ago and a time of innocence and hope. For just a moment he was able to relive that time of curiosity and wonderment at the world. But just as quickly, it went away. What happened instead was that flash of memory that seemed to distort whatever he remembered into shaky, blurred images.

Sometimes he felt like he didn't remember anything and other times he could recount an obscure event from long ago. The doctors had told him this would continue to happen. But it seemed to be getting worse lately.

"You boys can set up these firepots along the other side." He pointed to a wooden crate nearby containing a dozen firepots.

Matthew was just starting to run when Nicodemus shouted after him.

"Slow down, go easy, no need to fall and hurt yourselves. And be careful with them, they have kerosene inside and you don't want to spill it." Nicodemus added.

Matthew and Bernie knelt down and grabbed two firepots. They were heavier than the two expected, heavy enough for each to carry only one. Matthew remembered seeing these at Simpson's store but never really knew what they were. They were painted in army green with stenciled writing on the side.

"This is real army stuff," Bernie said as they walked to the other side of the path. "Like in the war." Matthew felt it wasn't necessary to dwell on this, they were doing a job and they had responsibility.

When they reached the right spot across from the first firepot that Nicodemus had set down, Matthew lay his firepot down gently. He made sure that it was in the same position as the other one across the path.

Then he measured off five feet by walking five steps and pointed where the next firepot should be placed.

"I know," said Bernie firmly.

Nicodemus watched them from the platform which was still not completely finished. He thought about what he was doing building this thing in his field that he really couldn't explain to anyone.

It could be the work of a madman he thought, in fact he figured most of the town thought that of him already. But they didn't have his pain and his hurt and his loneliness and they didn't know what he wanted. That the time had come for him to do this. That soon they would know and everyone would know that he was right.

He also realized that somehow Matthew was part of it. He wasn't sure how or why but the boy was part of this whole thing. He looked up at the elevators, towering above them and he knew they were also part of what was going to happen. And for just a moment it seemed like he could see a face on the side of one elevator. If you looked hard it almost seemed like the face of a woman. Then it was disappeared in shadows.

Matthew and Bernie continued to place the firepots along the pathway. By now they were moving quickly and when Bernie tripped and fell, he hadn't noticed that his firepot hit a rock and cracked ever so slightly.

Matthew looked at Bernie with a parental face, shaking his head. Bernie stumbled back to his feet and picked up the cracked firepot not noticing that his hands had become slightly moist.

"Boy, these things sure smell," Bernie said as he placed the last firepot down. "It's the kerosene," Matthew said, sounding so official. They stood back and looked at their work. One long and very neat row of firepots that complemented the other side of the path. Nicodemus now stood up and looked down the path and the boys work.

"Looks good," answered Nicodemus.

Bernie nodded then looked at his watch. It was nearing seven o'clock. A sudden thought came to him.

"Can we light them?"

Again Matthew gave Bernie that look that said he shouldn't push too far. But Bernie was determined.

"I have to go home soon and I just want to see them all lighted." This time Matthew secretly shared Bernie's wish and turned to Nicodemus.

He wouldn't say anything but he hoped Nicodemus would light them.

Nicodemus looked down the row of firepots and considered it. It was too soon to do this as the sun was barely setting on the horizon. But yet he shared the excitement of seeing the firepots all light and glowing in the soft twilight. It was that excitement that pushed Nicodemus to start lighting the firepots as Matthew and Bernie stood back.

He flicked his old Ronson lighter onto the wick of the first firepot. It took a few seconds and caught, flickering then lighting up like a big candle. He lit the second one and the third and continued until he came to the end. Then he lit the last one, the one Bernie had accidentally cracked.

The wick flickered just a little then lit up. Nicodemus stepped away and crossed over to the other side and began lighting them as well. Bernie and Matthew stood back, watching as the pathway became a magical runway in the field. But Bernie also noticed something else, something that didn't mean much a few moments before. His hand smelled of kerosene. He raised it to his nose then to his mouth and tasted it. It was bitter and he spit it out. Bernie suddenly had a terrifying thought.

"Matthew…"

But it was too late. The cracked firepot suddenly exploded into a small fireball with incredible force. It was enough to blast the firepot into a hundred pieces, scattering them in a circle of twenty feet. Not enough to hurt either of the three, but enough to start a fire in the dry stubble of the wheat field that Nicodemus had cut.

Nicodemus immediately went into action. First he ran to the boys who stood stunned but unhurt.

"Stand back," he shouted. Then he ran to the platform and grabbed a shovel and ran to the fire trying to beat it out. But it was clearly a losing battle. The fire spread quickly following the trail of kerosene that had leaked.

Nicodemus was quick to push away the other firepots extinguishing them the best he could. But now the fire was going in different directions following the spew of kerosene and even he wasn't able to fight every fire. Something drastic had to be done as he looked at the two boys.

"Matthew!" He shouted. "Matthew, go to the fire hall and turn on the alarm, break the glass. Both of you!"

Matthew and Bernie stood there without moving. Neither knew what to do.

"Matthew, Bernie! GO!"

Matthew suddenly snapped out of his daze and ran to his bike. Bernie followed and they both pedaled as fast as they could towards Main Street. Nicodemus then ran to the elevator, kicking out small fires as he went. He pushed the office door open and disappeared inside then came out with a large portable fire extinguisher. There were now several trails of fire, some going towards the wheat field, others coming towards the elevators. Nicodemus knew the consequences of a fire near the elevator. With the thousands of bushels of wheat stored inside came a liability, the air was filled with wheat dust which was as combustible as gunpowder. And Nicodemus knew something else. If the fire reached the elevator it could blow the entire ten story structure into dust.

It took the boys less than two minutes to reach the firehall. The small building was closed and nobody was there as it was a volunteer fire department. Matthew arrived first and ran to the door knocking.

"Nobody's there, you gotta ring the alarm," shouted Bernie.

"Where is it," Matthew shouted back.

"I don't know," answered Bernie.

Both boys ran up and down the front of the building looking for the fire alarm. Matthew finally spotted it on a pole near the firehall. It was a glass-covered box with a small hammer on a chain.

"Hit it," Bernie yelled.

Matthew lifted the hammer and, closing his eyes, smashed the glass, hitting the pad inside. For a second nothing happened. Then the fire alarm blasted a shrill scream louder than anything Matthew had ever heard. The siren was certainly enough to wake the whole town and it wasn't long before the first volunteer arrived.

25

The fire actually hadn't done that much damage and by the time the town's aging fire engine arrived Nicodemus had pretty much put it out.

Black smoke smoldered as the fire hose sprayed over one of the few areas still hot.

Matthew was there with Bernie, both watching the fire engine. The dozen or more townspeople had already begun heading back to their homes. Loading the fire engine hoses and equipment were Simpson, Lorne, Anderson, and Mr. Bernstein. They spoke in hushed voices and now and then and would glance over at Nicodemus sitting on the platform.

Bernie looked incredibly guilty knowing full well that his mistake had caused the fire. The fire was out but there was still the issue of a whole town waking and the fire department bringing the fire engine now.

"Now I'm really in trouble," Bernie spoke lightly.

"It was an accident, Bernie," Matthew said, "And it got put out."

"But I did it, I dropped that firepot thing," Bernie answered.

But before they could volunteer any more, Simpson began to walk over to Nicodemus. Nicodemus wasn't looking at him but he could sense Simpson approaching and he knew it was trouble.

"Nicodemus," Simpson spoke in a low growling tone.

Nicodemus looked first at Matthew and Bernie.

"When the hell you gonna learn to protect these buildings. If that fire hit the elevators... this whole town could blow sky high. Just what the hell are you building there, Nicodemus?"

Nicodemus turned to Simpson and the others. "It was just an accident, one of the firepots you sold me was flawed," Nicodemus said as he glanced over at Bernie and Matthew. "The fire is out, nothing got burned, there's nothing else to say."

Matthew knew in that instant that Nicodemus was covering for Bernie. He turned to Bernie who knew it as well.

"You're forgetting I'm the police in Empire," Simpson said.

Nicodemus didn't answer. As Lorne and the Reverend approached, Simpson looked at the firepots, something was connecting and it was something very surprising.

"If I didn't know any better..." Simpson started.

"What?" Lorne asked.

In the war, we used to make temporary airfields for supply planes to land", Simpson answered. "We'd set patterns just like that."

"You saying he's making an airplane landing strip?" Lorne asked.

"It's too short for an airplane," Simpson added.

Lorne smiled and nodded towards Matthew and Bernie, "Maybe it's for flying saucers."

The Reverend, who had been quiet all this time now found a place to lend his own opinion. "Those circles are the work of a greater power than we know."

"Now don't go putting the fear of God into everyone, Reverend," Simpson said. But the Reverend wasn't finished yet as he turned to Simpson, "What do you expect... all this flying saucer talk. It's blasphemy, that's what it is."

Lorne approached Nicodemus slowly and leaned on the platform.

"What is this Nicodemus?"

Nicodemus knew that Lorne was the friendliest of all these men. He would even say hello to Nicodemus on the street or in a store. Sometimes Nicodemus wished he could talk to Lorne or the others for that matter. But whenever he tried it didn't seem to come out right. They just didn't understand him and probably never would.

"Nothing," was all Nicodemus said.

Simpson then turned to Nicodemus, "But you'd better not let anything happen here again or else I'll recommend to the grain agent that he find another caretaker."

With that the two men returned to the fire truck as Simpson stayed behind. He looked at the two boys.

"What are you two doing here?" he demanded.

Bernie's nervousness was still obvious. Simpson turned towards Nicodemus still sitting on the platform.

"You boys have anything to do with this fire?" he glared straight at Bernie, who looked the guiltiest.

"They had nothing to do with it," Nicodemus's voice answered from behind Simpson. Simpson turned to see Nicodemus who turned to the boys.

"I told you kids to go home so now get going," he said.

At that moment, Mr. Bernstein appeared, Simpson retreated and Bernie rushed over to his father's side and both of them left.

Matthew looked straight at Nicodemus. By now, Matthew knew some of Nicodemus's moods and he recognized what looked like a need for them to go. Finally he climbed on his bike and rode off. Simpson took one last look at the burned area.

"You make sure this fire is completely out, understand?" He said

Nicodemus nodded and watched as the men climbed onto the fire truck and drove away. When they were all gone, Nicodemus looked at the fire damage. Then a voice came from the shadows.

"Why'd you lie?" Matthew asked in a quiet tone.

26

Matthew stepped out from the shadows to confront Nicodemus. He had waited until the fire truck had gone. Bernie was probably already home but Matthew had questions and why Nicodemus took the blame for the fire was just the first. Now they both sat on the platform.

"Why'd you lie?" he repeated.

"Fire was an accident, don't matter how it started," Nicodemus answered. "Wasn't a lie."

Matthew sat there for a moment mulling it over in his mind. It was an accident, but when a kid has an accident with something like fire, it always seemed a bigger deal than when an adult had the same accident. Kids got punished. Adults rarely got anything for accidents at least as far as Matthew knew.

"Maybe I guess not then," said Matthew. Nicodemus took one of the tin cups and poured coffee for Matthew. He passed it to the boy then poured a cup for himself. Matthew lifted the cup to his mouth and sipped the strong coffee and once again failed his attempt to conceal the bitterness. This coffee drinking must take a long time to master he thought. He also remembered that he had questions.

"Nicodemus, what's it mean, your name?"

"It comes from the Bible," Nicodemus said as a memory flashed back to him and he held onto it as long as he could. "Nicodemus was an educated man and knew many languages, they say." Then, another memory flashed past. "My grandmother named me that."

"Did she live on Thunder Hill?" Matthew said quickly, hoping that Nicodemus was in the mood to talk more.

"What do you know about Thunder Hill?" Nicodemus said.

Matthew sipped more of the bitter black coffee and it took a moment to form his next words.

"I went there. I found the sign from the café," he said and without waiting for an answer he said, "What was it like there?"

Nicodemus leaned back, his mind finding memories that he hadn't thought for awhile. It was always different, the thought for a moment, memories would come and go. There was never a regular pattern but yet when the boy asked it seemed like it was easier to find those memories.

"It was a fine town in it's time," he started, "We had farms, stores, even the cafe. If a fellow wanted an ice-cream cone, he'd go right down to the cafe and have it, without no problems."

Why would you have problems getting ice cream?" Matthew asked.

"We were a little different from most folks," Nicodemus answered reluctantly.

"How?"

"Different." The tone of his voice was more permanent this time and Matthew figured it best to move away from that particular question.

"I saw a newspaper there," he said changing the subject a little bit, hopefully enough that he could get Nicodemus to continue talking. "It had pictures like the one you have. Soldiers going to war."

Nicodemus thought for a moment, he wondered why the memories continued to flow and he decided to keep going. "One day an army recruiter came to town and told us about this war across the ocean," he said, "And that we had to fight for freedom. Most all the eligible men joined up and went off, me included. Trouble is most of them was killed in places you probably never heard of. The ones that survived, some ended up in the cities and some like me, in veteran hospitals."

"I didn't know you were in a hospital," Matthew said.

"I wasn't for long."

Matthew felt that his answer was another one of those that would have to be enough.

"What happened to the town?" he asked carefully watching Nicodemus's face.

"Without the men to work the fields and the businesses it started dying." He answered. "Some of the women did a damn good job of it but eventually, the town just plain lost it's will to live. The ones that were left, the women an' children and old ones, they moved to other places."

"Like your Mary," Matthew said carefully.

"Like my Mary," Nicodemus smiled.

"Where'd she go?"

Nicodemus shifted and looked straight ahead. The memories of Mary always had a particularly hard time coming back. Sometimes he'd stare at the photograph in the house for a long time hoping to bring back something that he could remember. But it rarely came back. Many times he wondered about what they said to each other, the words that were exchanged after a hard day's work as they both watched the sunset. But the memory of the words never came back.

"Far away," was all he could come up with, "Too far." Then Nicodemus stood up and climbed down off the platform. "Best be you go on home now, Matthew, your mama's gonna be worried about you."

Matthew knew the question period was over, at least for now. But he had one burning question left, one that he had been trying to form since he had become friends with Nicodemus. Now the words ran in his head, spinning into a dozen combinations until finally they came out.

"Did you know my dad?"

Nicodemus seemed to ponder that for a moment, but Matthew really wasn't sure as it was hard to read him and his moods at the best of times.

"No," was all he said. Then, "g'night."

Nicodemus walked back to his home leaving Matthew alone on the platform. Matthew sat there for a moment, looking all around. Then his eyes rose towards the darkening sky and he stared up at the first stars twinkling millions of miles away from him and he wondered like we all do what was up there.

And almost as if to answer, a falling star raced across the nearly black sky until it disintegrated in the atmosphere.

To anyone else it would have been a meteorite, to Matthew it was a sign.

27

The newspaper headline read UFO OVER LOS ANGELES and a smaller headline near the bottom said SAUCER SEEN IN CALGARY. Matthew stared at the newspaper on the small rack in the grocery store. Since Empire had only a weekly newspaper the grocer also carried a few out-of-town newspapers that were usually bought by businessmen. Another newspaper had a small headline saying WAITING FOR THE EMPEROR.

Matthew had been up early and he was the first one on Main Street. But there was nothing much to see as it was too early for anyone to be there. The only business that was open was Sam's cafe, and even that was barely open. By the time he got home, Elana had asked him to get some milk from the grocery store.

On his way to the store, which had just opened, he noticed several people leaving with big bags of groceries. It was unusual for townspeople to shop this early, usually shopping in Empire was later in the day and mostly on Saturdays.

But this morning, as Matthew had entered the store and it was bustling with business. So busy in fact that all the milk was gone. Matthew had never seen it when all the milk was gone.

Then he noticed that some of the shelves that held canned goods were empty. Then Simpson appeared carrying two armfuls of groceries and pushing along the grocer's son who was carrying two more bags of groceries to Simpson's truck.

Matthew noticed the grocer and the cashier watching and whispering something to each other.

Outside on Main Street Matthew's classmate Paul, wearing a space helmet, chased a girl with his Rocket Blaster water pistol until two bigger girls ambushed him with their own Rocket Blasters.

Matthew watched them run down the street as he tried to figure out why everyone was acting so strange. A poster on a telephone pole featured a "Martian Hop," with a local rock and roll band who had renamed themselvesThe 5 Martians. For Matthew it seemed like everyone in town had been possessed by some strange power like in those serials he saw at the movie theater. There was also something disturbing about it, something he felt was wrong.

Across town Nicodemus was finishing work on the platform as Miss Major approached. He had seen her coming but waited to acknowledge her until she was almost there.

"Come to see the crazy man in town?" Nicodemus said.

"I came to see what the fuss is," she said as she looked at the platform and the pathway. There was also wiring leading up to the elevators. She studied the construction site for a moment.

"Well, you sure did stir up the town," she continued. "You and Matthew. Talk is going on about Martians all across the valley." Then she looked directly at Nicodemus.

"Do you really think something is going to happen here?"

Nicodemus stood up and faced her.

"Not up to me."

She paced around, a little apprehensive.

"I don't think any spacemen are coming her to this field or this town," she said matter-of-factly.

Nicodemus knew he couldn't tell her everything. In fact he wasn't sure about this whole thing and he certainly couldn't tell her about the visions he had recently, about lights from the sky and flashes of Mary. It was enough that the town thought he was crazy, he didn't want her believing it either.

"Probably not," he answered, hoping he sounded normal. "You ever read George Orwell? When is two plus two not four?"

Miss Major smiled, "When you don't want it to be."

Nicodemus nodded.

"So you're saying that the whole town is acting a little strange because they want to be, and that nothing is really going to happen?" Miss Major said curiously.

Suddenly Nicodemus seemed to lose any more words he could say to her. And what was worse, she could see it in his face and she knew too. Still, she wanted to stay there and talk to him but something was different. Now she wasn't so sure about him. And it was time to go.

"I have homework to correct. Assuming the world will be safe tomorrow." She said.

"Of course," Nicodemus said.

Miss Major turned and left. Nicodemus watched her until she walked out of sight. Then he went back to finishing the platform. He had learned a long time ago that when his mind was troubled work would help to ease the confusion.

Most of the day remained unusually strange for Matthew. He had noticed more townspeople acting peculiar. Some whispered to each other and others ran from store to store buying all sorts of goods. School seemed okay but Matthew sensed a tension in the air. It was like Miss Major was talking but she was thinking about something else. Some of the other kids seemed to be similarly preoccupied. Even Bernie was distant today, staring off for long periods of time until Miss Major asked him to pay closer attention. It was a room of people whose minds were somewhere else.

It wasn't until early evening that Matthew and Bernie met on the roof of the hotel. They had agreed on that earlier in the day and Matthew hoped he could figure out what was happening to his town by then. Bernie fired his BB gun at a paper target with a space alien drawn in crayon. The BBs pierced the thin sheet of paper and Bernie cocked the gun and fired again. Matthew stood by the edge of the roof and scanned as much of the town as he could see with an old set of binoculars Bernie had taken from his dad's workshop. His own BB gun stood ready by his side. It wasn't new like Bernie's, in fact hardly anything of Matthew's was new. But he had gotten used to the old gun and its rusted metal barrel and scratched wood stock. Even though they both knew BB guns couldn't really stop anything, they somehow felt a little more secure with them.

"Nothing unusual," Matthew said as he lowered the binoculars.

"My dad said he might take mom and me up to the lake tomorrow," Bernie said as he looked out at the town.

"He can't," Matthew started, "Tomorrow is when it's gonna happen."

Bernie nodded, "It's my mom. She's scared about everything."

"But it's safer here with everybody."

Something was stirring in Bernie as he turned to Matthew.

"What makes you think the Emperor guy is gonna come here? It's not like we're important or anything."

"If he's gonna come, he's gonna come here."

However Bernie was thinking about something else, something that was delicate at the very least.

"Maybe he'll know about your dad?"

There was silence between them for a moment, this was dangerous territory for Bernie and he knew what the reaction could be. Still, he really wanted to know what Matthew was thinking. After all, they were best friends and if you couldn't ask a best friend a tough question then you really weren't best friends. Matthew thought about it for a moment and then spoke.

"You think so?"

"I don't know," Bernie answered, "If heaven's out there somewhere and the Emperor is from Mars, well, that's kind of out there too so maybe he's been there."

In the stillness of dusk for a moment anything was possible as both boys considered the possibilities that seemed too immense to even think about. Bernie found the way out. "Whattya think they'll have to eat at Stephanie's party?," he asked in all sincerity, "I hope they don't have that meat spread stuff that we had at Gloria's party in fourth grade."

They both turned to look at the town beneath them as the darkness of night slipped over them.

"I hope not too," answered Matthew. But he wasn't thinking about meat spread sandwiches. There was something bigger to think about. Tomorrow was the day he had written down in his scribbler. The day the Emperor of Mars would arrive.

28

The sun rose as a bright yellow and orange ball of fire that seemed to pour over the land. This was fitting for the day the Emperor of Mars would come to Empire. Matthew woke up with a start, so fast that he had almost forgotten his dream about spacemen and Nicodemus and Miss Major and even oddly enough Stephanie.

Matthew leapt out of bed and ran outside to see what was happening. As with most days in Empire nothing much was happening at all. The world was still there and the only life that Matthew could sense was the distant bark of a dog. Just then he realized why Stephanie had entered his dreams last night. The party. He wondered if he should go but knew he had to. After all the entire class was going before school was out.

An alien face leapt into view and a girl shrieked as a boy in a home-made alien costume chased her across the lawn at Simpson's house. It was Stephanie's party. They passed the

Martian drawing contest entries, all taped onto bristle board cards and exhibited like they were in an art gallery.

Not that anybody here had ever seen a real art gallery. That was except for Miss Major who was responsible for the display. The images were a collection of different styles and ideas, some were curious, others were interesting, some were just plain ordinary.

Matthew and Bernie made their way to a table prepared with food and drink for the kids. There was a selection of green and red finger sandwiches, the kind where the crusts were cut off and Bernie cautiously tasted one. The verdict was quick in coming.

"Meat spread," he said disappointedly. Then he looked around to see if anyone was looking and discretely took out the chewed sandwich in his mouth and looked for a waste basket. But none was to be seen so Bernie stuffed it into his pocket for later disposal. Both boys moved back from the table determined not to eat the sandwiches.

"Hi Bernie," purred Stephanie as she approached and then smiled at Matthew. "Hi, Matthew." Stephanie was dressed in her costume, best described as Space Princess.

"How do you like how I look?"

"Okay, I guess," Matthew said, casually looking around. He didn't want to even think that he'd mention the dream with Stephanie in it. She would drag that out for the rest of Grade 6. And besides, he had forgotten the dream anyways after waking up so fast.

"Have you seen my drawing?" She asked. And before they could answer she took both boys by the arm and brought them over to her drawing which was very precise and colorful as it portrayed a flying saucer with what could best be described as cute aliens. Matthew just shook his head.

"Do you like it?"

"It's okay." Matthew answered, turning his head, looking for an escape. That's when he spotted Miss Major talking with Mrs. Simpson. Matthew didn't notice that Bernie had managed to sneak away as Stephanie gave all her attention to him.

"Where's your picture?" she asked softly.

"Don't have one."

"Why not?"

"I don't know what he looks like," Matthew answered as he noticed something odd. Simpson appeared, carrying big wood boxes around to the back of his house. It would be perfectly normal except for the glances Simpson made that seemed to suggest he was doing something very secret. But maybe it was just Matthew's suspicion as everything today was becoming strange to him. All he could really think of was tonight and Nicodemus and the Emperor of Mars. All around him was a circus of bad drawings, people eating those funny sandwiches, girls giggling and boys teasing them. Didn't they know what was going to happen today, Matthew thought; didn't they know their life would be changed? And he also wondered what Mr. Simpson was doing.

"Where's your dad going?" he suddenly asked Stephanie.

"Oh, he's just putting stuff into the room in the cellar," she answered. " Have you had any of the punch? I made it." Stephanie took Matthew by the arm and dragged him back to the table where Gloria stood dressed in an expensive store-bought costume.

"Stephanie, this is simply a divine party," she said smugly.

"Thank you, Gloria," Stephanie replied.

The distraction was enough for Matthew to step away and as he turned he noticed more adults appearing at the party. This time it was Anderson, the Reverend and Lorne and they approached Mrs. Simpson and spoke to her. She said something and pointed them to the back of the house. The three men proceeded to go where Matthew had seen Simpson go earlier. Matthew wondered what they had talked about especially after noticing Mrs. Simpson whose smile had turned into a frown.

Behind the house, the three men waited until Simpson stepped out of the basement door. When he saw them, he stopped. He had the kind of look that you get when you've been caught with your hand in the cookie jar.

"Afternoon, Bill," Anderson said with a crisp tone.

"What's up?" Simpson grumbled.

"You stayin' around the house today?" Anderson prodded.

"Got things to do," Simpson said as he started to walk past them.

"You know, I never seen that bomb shelter of yours," Anderson said accusingly as he looked toward the basement door.

"Got no bomb shelter, told ya that," Simpson shot back.

But the three men exchanged looks that suggested neither of them believed it.

"We figure we got a right to see it," Lorne piped up. And Anderson continued, "See if it conforms to zoning laws."

"I'm on the town committee also, Andy," Simpson said in a loud voice, "In case you forgot. And like I said, there isn't anything there."

Matthew had escaped from Stephanie and Gloria and had just made it to the corner of the house where the men had gone. He leaned against the wall and listened. From here he could hear everything they said. And that was when someone touched him from behind causing him to jump. He whirled and turned, ready to tell Stephanie to leave him alone. But it wasn't Stephanie.

"Matthew. You haven't said a word to me the whole afternoon," said Miss Major as she stood smiling at him.

Matthew glanced back at where the four men were confronting something he desperately wanted to know. But now Miss Major stood in front of him. As he stumbled for words, Miss Major took him by the hand and led him back to the party. The shock of her holding his hand was enough to shake away any thoughts he might have had till then.

Right now there were only four people in the world, his mother, Bernie, Nicodemus and Miss Major. He would consider forgiving her talking to Nicodemus on her own.

"Come with me, I have a special job for you," she said as she took Matthew to the alien picture display.

They passed Bernie who noticed her hand holding Matthew's and he winked at Matthew with an accompanying nod.

Stephanie also watched Miss Major lead Matthew and couldn't help but be a little envious of her. But what was worse was Matthew's look of complete helplessness. Boys, who knew what they thought, she wondered. Miss Major let Matthew's hand go as she motioned with both hands for the class to gather.

"Class, this is certainly turning out to be a wonderful party, isn't it?" she said.

"Yes, Miss Major," the class replied in broken unison. "I think we have to express our thanks to Stephanie and her mother, Mrs. Simpson, for the nice food and everything else," she continued, "Together."

"Thank you Mrs. Simpson and Stephanie," the class chimed together, again in their usual broken unison.

Miss Major pulled Matthew closer to her, brushing against her side.

"And, I thought we should all thank Matthew for bringing the Martian story to our attention," she said smiling at him. "It certainly has become a big event around town."

Just as Matthew was glowing in the warm light of Miss Major and the class, raised adult voices suddenly interrupted the moment and everyone turned towards the house to see Simpson and the three men walk into view.

"Damn it, Tom," Simpson was suddenly shouting, "Nobody tells me what I can or can't do. You understand?"

The class became suddenly silent. Dolores Anderson had a worried look on her face as Miss Major glanced over at Mrs. Simpson. Matthew's attention focused on the men.

"You can't keep that place a secret anymore," Anderson said angrily. "We all got the right to know."

"You got no right to be on my property!" Simpson yelled back.

The tension was rising and the kids stood perfectly still with more than a sense of uncertainty and apprehension.

"This ain't the army, Bill," Anderson replied, "you can't go around ordering me like I was some buck private. We're gonna vote on this... this thing."

"You're not gonna do anything, you damn fool," Simpson shouted even louder.

"You got a bomb shelter there and you've been stocking up food like a packrat," Anderson shot back. "We got a right to know about it."

Simpson suddenly shoved Anderson hard enough for him to stumble back. This was turning into something very serious in front of the kids who watched with eyes wide open, not sure what would happen next. Mrs. Simpson came up to her husband and tried to pull him away but he pushed her back. Matthew glanced at Stephanie who looked very scared as her mother again tried to calm Simpson. Then Anderson stepped between them and pushed Simpson back. Simpson suddenly swung his fist, connecting a solid hit in Anderson's face.

"Daddy!" Dolores screamed.

Anderson fell to the ground and got up slowly as the other men and Mrs. Simpson tried to keep Simpson from going at him again.

"That's it, Bill," Anderson said, tasting the blood in his mouth. "That's it!"

Mrs. Simpson suddenly took over, facing all of the men. "All four of you, just stop this, stop this now," she said loudly. Then she looked over at the class, "The children are watching, for heaven's sake." For Matthew and Bernie, it was the first time they saw men fighting for real, men who were fathers. They, like the rest of the class, were silent, waiting for what would happen next.

It was only then that the four men cooled enough to realize the class was watching. Dolores ran to her father as Simpson stomped off. Stephanie turned and ran to the house, crying.

"Wow I never saw a grownup hit anyone in real life," Bernie said as he appeared next to Matthew. "It's not like the movies, is it?"

"No," said Matthew quietly as he watched Miss Major begin to round up the class. The party was over.

"Guess this means we won't get any cake," Bernie shrugged.

Matthew wasn't thinking of cake at this moment. Somehow this day was fated to be strange, he figured. There was something very disturbing about the fight with the adults to him. It was different than Tommy and his bully friends, that was kid stuff. But when adults fought it carried with it a feeling of seriousness and hurt and Matthew didn't like that at all.

But the day wasn't over yet as Matthew's look followed the men as they left the yard and walked down the street.

Far down the street the elevators stood out against the sky with an almost ominous feeling to them. Matthew suddenly remembered what else was going to happen today. He looked at his Gene Autry wristwatch. It was late afternoon. Something bigger was going to happen.

29

Later that day, Matthew was the only living soul as he rode his bike down the center of Main Street. Not a single other resident of Empire could be seen. The silence was almost deafening as his wheels click-clacked on the pavement. The only time he'd ever seen it like this was on Sunday mornings but even then there would be a car or truck parked somewhere. Today the street was empty.

When he arrived at the café he was surprised to see the OPEN sign lit up. And sure enough, inside at his chair, Sam waited for business. One thing about Sam, he was never closed, even if the world were to end.

Matthew finally arrived at home and parked his bike against the wall. He took another look around the neighborhood but nothing stirred. It was as though everyone in town had left and he was all alone. As he walked to the kitchen door he wondered if his mother and grandmother would be there. For all he knew there was nobody except him. He wondered about Bernie and if he and his parents had left for safer ground.

It was hard to believe that two weeks had passed so quickly since he had heard the radio message from the Emperor of Mars and his promise to come to Earth to reveal the secrets of the universe. And he remembered how everyone laughed at him. But now nobody was laughing, nobody was around, not Tommy, not Simpson, not Lorne, not even Miss Major.

For a moment Matthew considered going to her second floor apartment to see if she was okay but reminded himself that he had to plan for the evening and that Nicodemus would need him more.

Nicodemus.

He suddenly realized he hadn't thought about Nicodemus for a long time. They were partners now in the landing pad for the Emperor. That's what it was, that's what it always was even when Simpson and the others were guessing Matthew knew. Even when Nicodemus's vague answers gave little clues Matthew knew. The Emperor would be landing tonight.

Matthew stepped into the kitchen prepared to see an empty house. Instead, Elana looked up at him from the stove. She smiled and it made Matthew feel better. He was not alone. They ate in silence and Matthew glanced at the clock as the hours approached 6 pm. Once in a while Elana caught his look and Matthew quickly turned his attention to the comic book spread out by his plate. Finally he finished eating. Babka also finished and left to go to her room and pray. Matthew and Elana were alone.

"Mom, I'm finished," Matthew said carefully. "Can I go now?"

"Matthew, you eat too fast."

"I gotta go see."

"There's nothing to see. You can stay home for one night."

"But..," Matthew pleaded.

"You can stay home tonight!" Elana said forcefully.

Matthew kicked at his chair. "It's not fair. I gotta be at Nicodemus's tonight. I gotta be there, mom. Please."

Elana was firm, "Go to your room and study for school."

Matthew suddenly threw his comic book away. He glared at her.

"I hate you. I wish I was with dad!"

The words surprised Matthew as much as Elana. He had never said that before, had never even thought it. But there it was, there was no going back now. Matthew rose up quickly and ran to his room slamming the door behind him.

Elana did not make an effort to go after him. She just sat there with a sad look on her face. She didn't like being as forceful as she was with him but she like many others in town was afraid. This Emperor thing might be just foolish, she thought, and surely the leaders of her town or her country would have spoken on this matter if it really were true. But still Elana had seen how the town had changed in the last week and how people began to speak less to their friends and neighbors. Now she looked over at Babka praying as she always did and Elana wondered about her life and that of her young fatherless son. She worked hard for the little money they had and she knew that her husband's mother did not care especially for her or Matthew. Elana disliked the entitled obligation the old woman expected of her and that she felt Elana was somehow responsible for her son's death in Europe. Yet Elana knew she had to continue to look after the old woman because that was what was done with her people. Elana glanced at Matthew's door and considered talking to him. But she would wait a little more to allow him his grief and his anger.

Matthew lay on his bed, looking up at the movie posters all the while thinking. By now he had already been sorry for telling Elana he hated her. He didn't know why he had said it and he wasn't sure how to tell her he was sorry. Yet there was a more urgent thought in his head as he looked at his second-hand clock. It was nearing seven o'clock. Matthew suddenly jumped up, walked to his closet and pulled out his BB gun. He reached for several plastic bags of brass-colored BBs and stuffed them into his pocket. He had a mission stronger than anything he'd ever felt in his life and he knew where he had to be. Matthew walked to the window and lifted it just a crack. It squeaked. He slowly lifted it higher until there was room enough for him to crawl outside.

Setting his BB gun ahead of him first, Matthew slipped outside into the twilight.

30

When Matthew arrived at Nicodemus's on his bike the sun was just beginning to reach the horizon, changing the blue sky into a softer blue hue. The air was cooling and night would come soon. As he set the bike down Matthew noticed that Nicodemus had placed his two chairs and the rocking chair on the platform. The photograph of Mary stood on the trunk which also had been moved onto the platform. Nicodemus was lighting the firepots and he continued as Matthew walked up to him.

"Come for the show?" Nicodemus said without looking at him.

Matthew knew what his answer was, "I came to see the Emperor of Mars."

"There's no Emperor of Mars. There isn't anything on Mars."

"Then why did we build this?"

Nicodemus stopped lighting the firepots for a moment and he stood up, stretched and looked back towards the crop circle. "Because something inside of me has been telling me to build it since that storm. Can't explain it, just know I got to do it. Like the ducks that fly south, you know?"

"That's what makes me want to be here too," Matthew said. And then he added, "Like the ducks."

Near the elevator a truck stopped and two people inside watched quietly. They were townspeople and the look on their faces was one of apprehension and curiosity. They weren't sure why they came there but they knew they had to come. And right now they were satisfied just by watching the man and the young boy and the crop circle and the firepots.

Nobody else showed up for at least a half hour but as dusk began to crawl across the open prairie like a dark shadow creature and the eastern sky became a horizon of purple more towners came. Two young men drove up in a car. They got out and leaned against the fender of the car and watched, drinking bottles of soda pop. Their car radio was playing rock and roll from the distant radio station. Two young teens arrived and sat on the railroad tracks, joking and pushing each other so that the other would fall.

By this time the firepots were all lit and Nicodemus and Matthew stood back to look at the trail behind them, leading back from the elevators to the crop circle and the platform. Neither Matthew nor Nicodemus took any time to look at the townspeople, they still had more work to do. Nicodemus looked up at the elevators that stood against the darkening sky.

Across town, Simpson looked outside the window of his house unsure of what he would see. But there was nothing and there had been nobody on his street for hours now. It was unusual but sometimes unusual things happened. Yet there was a hint of uneasiness in his eyes even though he wouldn't have admitted it to anyone. He turned back to his family. A radio crackled with music as Mrs. Simpson, Tommy and Stephanie ate silently in the dining room. Simpson walked over to his chair at the head of the table and sat down. He glanced towards the wall where a loaded rifle leaned. As he turned he caught Mrs. Simpson looking at him and it was clear she wasn't happy about the firearm in their presence.

At the movie theater, the outside lights came on, lighting up a poster for a war movie. Yet no customers appeared at the box office.

In Bernstein's lobby the TV set was on even though nobody was there watching. Mr. Bernstein entered and looked around. He turned to see Mrs. Bernstein standing behind him in the doorway. They hadn't left town after all. It had taken him most of last night to convince his wife that nothing was going to happen to them or to anybody. In spite of that she still looked worried. Bernie entered and Mrs. Bernstein pulled him to her side and held him tightly. Bernie managed to give his father a squeezed look and a shrug.

Miss Major was marking test papers when she realized how quiet it was outside. She walked to her window and looked down at the empty street. A second or two of doubt crossed her mind, but she wiped it away with a smile. Still, there was an underlying feeling that drew her back to the window and the darkening sky above.

Under the elevators, Nicodemus walked to a power pole where he had connected extension cords that led upwards to the tops of the elevators. He looked at Matthew who stood by the firepot path watching and waiting. Then Nicodemus flicked a light switch.

Suddenly rows of Christmas lights lit up from the top of the elevators to the bottom. There were twinkling lights of blues, reds and greens, visible for at least a few miles. If you were a Martian and you were flying by in your flying saucer, you couldn't miss them. These lights would not present a fire danger as they were used every year for Christmas and not near enough to the storage bins. Besides, Nicodemus had them all in a single connection, meaning he could turn all of them off in a second, if need be.

By now the townspeople who arrived numbered about 30 looked up in awe. While they may have seen the lights at Christmas, they had never seen them in the configuration Nicodemus created.

Some gasped, others clapped, some just stood there silently.

On the roof of the hotel, Bernie could see the lights come on and he wished he could be there. He had to promise his mother he would not leave the hotel but the promise was getting harder and harder to keep. He looked at his BB gun leaning against the edge and checked his pocket for extra bags of BBs. Like Matthew he didn't think that BBs would do much of anything to stop a sparrow let alone a spaceman. But it brought some comfort to him and he decided he had to go to Matthew. Bernie walked over to the fire escape which led down to the ground. His parents would never see him leave. He started down.

At Nicodemus's place, Sam Wong had carefully set up a folding table where he offered paper cups of coffee and donuts and sandwiches to the townspeople. Not far away two enterprising 10-year olds were selling glasses of Kool Aid for 5 cents each.

Bernie passed by Sam and the kids as he walked from the elevator towards the path leading to the platform where Matthew and Nicodemus were finishing work. Matthew turned to see his friend carrying his BB gun.

"We didn't go," Bernie said before Matthew could ask. "I sneaked out. Dad's gonna kill me if he finds out."

"You can join us."

Bernie took the final steps towards the platform and stepped up onto it. They all sat down at the same time with Nicodemus taking the rocker.

"What are we doing?" Bernie asked.

"Waiting," Matthew said.

"Oh. Yeah," Bernie replied. Then he cocked his BB gun to make sure it was ready and he set it down beside him.

As the crowd grew, Miss Major appeared amongst them. She was fascinated by the growing crowd and was surprised that so many had come out. But then she knew small towns and certainly she had heard all the rumors about the Emperor of Mars. Yet it seemed incredible to her that people would want to believe that something as absurd as that, there was no Emperor of Mars, she was sure of that. Like Elana she knew that if there were, the government would certainly know about it, they had radar and all those kind of things that would no doubt shoot down anything that wasn't theirs. Men, she thought, always ready to shoot first then ask questions later. Yet there was something mysterious and almost inspiring about all this.

It was like a religion, she thought, and she remembered her Sunday school classes which she never liked going to. The ministers and priests would always talk about faith which had to suffice when material proof was not possible. You had to have faith in order to believe. And as she looked around at the others she realized many of them wanted faith and wanted to believe in something. And this was as good as anything else tonight.

Stephanie and her mother sat quietly in the living room as Simpson listened to a news report on the radio.

There was a brief story about the so-called Emperor of Mars and that so far there was no sign of him or his flying saucer. It gave neither relief nor fear to Simpson, and his family remained silent. Stephanie looked out the window as the sky grew darker. Soon it would be night. She knew where Matthew was and she wanted to go there to see him. But her father's orders were clear. Nobody left the house. And he had made them practice running down to that cellar room that had caused the fight between Simpson and Anderson during her party. The party that was spoiled forever.

But nobody noticed Tommy who had slipped quietly out of the kitchen, stopping only to take a set of keys that hung from a hook near the door.

Back at Nicodemus's place, a larger crowd had gathered, now over a hundred people. They had kept back from Nicodemus's field and the firepot path as though it might interfere with something. What that something was nobody knew for certain, but for now they were comfortable sitting and standing near the elevators just a stone's throw from the firepot path.

The same radio announcer mentioned the Emperor of Mars once again and then gave a weather report for tomorrow. Then just as music began to play something happened.

"Up there! Look! Up there!" a man in the crowd shouted.

Everyone heard it. People looked at each other, at the elevators, at the crop circles. And many looked up at the sky.

Another voice shouted, a woman's, "Over there! In the west!"

There, high in the western sky, something sparkled in the night. Something big.

31

"It's a star. That's all," shouted a man's voice. Another voice interrupted, "It ain't no star. Look how bright it is." Yet a third voice chimed in, "It's an airplane."

The Reverend looked at the bright light in the sky and shook his head. A farmer said "Ain't nobody got an airplane 'round here."

Bernie pulled out his binoculars and handed them to Matthew who focused on the light. It seemed to be unusually large but it wasn't doing much. In fact it was just sitting there high in the sky sparkling as the last warm colors of day faded to night.

"Is it him?" Bernie whispered.

"I don't think so," Matthew said as he watched the light.

"It's only Venus," Nicodemus interrupted, "It's always the first star to come out every night."

The word passed around the crowd, whispers of Venus and first star and every night mumbled and twisted through them. "What is the matter with all of you!" The Reverend suddenly shouted. They turned to him and waited. Even Miss Major watched him.

"There are no Martians, no aliens," he said with even more volume than before.

The crowd whispered a little and waited. He was finished now. His job had been done. He had put the fury of his preaching into them and surely they would go home.

"Look at the stars!" A woman shouted. And all eyes turned again to the sky and away from the Reverend. Again he shook his head realizing that he had not yet made them believe his version. In the sky, other stars began appearing, sparkling.

"It's stars," Bernie said disappointed. "That's all. Just stars."

Elana was not looking at the stars that very moment. She was looking into Matthew's room to see it empty. Behind her Babka stared at Elana with that look that she disliked so much. That look was the one that said in no uncertain terms, *can't you make your own child obey his mother?* It was one of many condescending looks Babka had and sometimes Elana wanted to tell her what she thought and that Matthew was not a bad boy. He was imaginative, that was certain but her husband, Babka's son, he had also been imaginative, a dreamer, a devoted man.

But she knew she had to find him. Her instincts as a mother told her she had to go to where Matthew would likely be if only to confirm that he was all right. The issue of leaving his room would come later.

There were upwards of a hundred townspeople at Nicodemus's place by now. Darkness had fallen and people used kerosene lamps, flashlights and even truck headlights to light the area between the elevators and Nicodemus's landing pad. With the initial scare over with and the Reverend keeping to himself they relaxed and waited for something else to happen.

The mood was almost festive as people laughed and joked and talked to each other. Some of them had met old friends or neighbors and talked about their crops and their jobs or they exchanged recipes and gossip.

Matthew carried coffee for himself and Bernie from Sam's coffee stand who gave it free to Matthew because he felt that Nicodemus's mysterious landing pad was making him money. Matthew had almost reached the firepot path when he heard his name called.

"Matthew."

He turned to see Miss Major approaching him. Matthew decided to keep walking, he didn't want the coffee to get cold. But he knew it was more than that. He was still a little upset at her. But she joined him and they walked side by side.

"There certainly is a crowd, isn't there," she said.

"They've come to see the Emperor," Matthew said without turning to her. She stepped in front of him and he had to stop.

"Matthew, sometimes people believe what they want to even when it isn't true," she said.

"Like you being mushy with Nicodemus?"

His look said it all. She never even thought of that, but realized he had seen her at the cafe with Nicodemus.

And she realized that the childhood crush she knew he had was quite serious in his world. She had forgotten how crushes worked, it had been so long since she took to liking a teacher in grade school.

She even remembered one, Mr. Hornbeck, he was young and handsome and all the girls talked about him behind his back. Now it was her turn to be the object of childhood fantasies. She knew she had to handle this matter delicately and honestly.

"I know you like me, Matthew," she started. "I like you too. But that was different. I think you understand that."

"Nicodemus is my friend," he said with narrowed eyes

"He still is. Nothing's changed." She said. "We're both your friends."

"Do you love him?" Matthew said quietly.

Miss Major wasn't expecting that and it caught her off guard and that tiny second of hesitation was seen as clear as a bell by Matthew who watched her eyes.

"He's been to so many places, even Paris. I like talking to him, that's all," she answered. It was more of an answer to herself than to Matthew.

She knew Nicodemus was different and that was what attracted her to him. Yet there was another side of him that made her keep her distance. There was a dark side, a piece of him that carried demons unlike anything she had known and she wasn't sure she wanted to know them.

"He knows the Emperor is coming," Matthew said Miss Major knelt down to his level, looking him eye to eye.

"I know this Emperor is important to you. Sometimes people think there's answers in the unknown, sometimes when they can't figure life out, they look to something that they can't explain. It makes them feel better."

Matthew looked at her and shook his head.

"Don't be disappointed if your Emperor doesn't show up," she continued. "You've got a lifetime ahead of you to see so many more things, things that are real and beautiful and wonderful."

There was only one thing left that Matthew wanted to ask and this seemed as good a time as any.

"Then you still like me?" He said shyly.

"Of course I like you. I care a lot about you, Matthew," she smiled, "I think you're going to do something important with your life." There was a silence between them. A truce had been bargained. There was no need for treaties or words, it was quietly understood by both of them.

"I gotta go," he said, smiling.

Then Miss Major did the most incredible thing. She leaned forward and kissed him ever so lightly on his forehead. Then she stood up.

"You're a very special boy, Matthew."

Matthew was shaken, she just kissed him.

Not from his mother or some old lady. It was real and his first ever of that kind. His hands shook as the coffee spilled. Then Matthew then did what any red-blooded boy of twelve would do. He ran away. Miss Major smiled to herself as she watched him run to the platform but she would never treat this lightly. She meant what she had said to him and she hoped that if, and that was a big if, if she ever got married and if she ever had children she would want a boy like Matthew. She might even call him Matthew. She thought about it so much she didn't notice three new arrivals.

Anderson, his wife and Dolores stepped out of his truck. They had anxious looks on their faces and they scanned the crowd until they saw the platform in the crop circle. Mrs. Anderson looked at her husband, her eyes were wide.

"Are you sure?" she asked.

"We have to do this," Anderson said sharply. "There's no other choice." And with that he led his wife and Dolores towards the firepot path and the platform at the end of it.

32

Matthew was the first to see Anderson and his family walk up the firepot path towards them. Up to now none of the townspeople had felt the inclination to walk onto the stubble-covered ground mostly because nobody else did. It was assumed that the path was there for a reason and the fact that the firepots on each side gave it more than a casual resemblance to an airport runway kept people away.

Anderson, his wife and Dolores reached the crop circle where the landing pad sat and he looked up at Nicodemus. "Nicodemus, since my missus here saw somethin' too, I figure we oughtta be here with ya," he said, "Somehow we become part of this thing whatever it is."

Matthew and Bernie turned to see how Nicodemus would react. He studied the family for a moment then casually said, "Do what you have to do."

Anderson sat on the platform as there were no more chairs. His wife and Dolores joined him. Now that they were there they didn't really know what to do. So they just sat. Dolores glanced up at Matthew who nodded to her in a very adult-like way. He realized he was copying Nicodemus's manner and attitude and was surprised at how it seemed to fit. Matthew wondered again about his father, that having an adult to watch and copy was part of that whole thing he had missed out on.

The crowd had gathered more and the festive mood continued as some watched the stars and others gossiped. Still others were silent, their eyes on the night sky looking for something that they weren't even sure if they'd recognize. Some of the townspeople began to move closer towards the path and the landing pad.

One of those moving closer was Nancy Carsen who had her eyes on Bernie as he sat on the raised platform. It took awhile for Bernie to notice her amongst the townspeople. Nancy smiled with her sparkling dark eyes and waved to him. Bernie was at first taken aback, unsure how to react. Then, with the confidence of his position as keeper of the third chair and part of the trio on the landing pad, Bernie nodded somewhat casually, acknowledging her. Then he turned back to watching the skies.

"Listen!" Someone shouted, "Everyone listen, the news!"

The crowd silenced itself as a car radio was turned up as loud as it could. Other radios also turned up and the echo of a dozen radios reverberated against the natural sound walls of the two elevators.

"...And finally," the broadcaster spoke, "Radio stations in the west who waited for the Martian broadcast set for tonight have reported no contact with the alleged Emperor of Mars, now well past his scheduled time of appearance. The Mars hoax originated in California when a group of outer space enthusiasts produced a tape recording which played a message from Mon-Ka, the Emperor of Mars, set to appear tonight."

The crowd continued to stand in silence but already some of the townspeople were exchanging looks and whispering. It didn't take long for whispers to become louder.

"While a number of UFO reports have been made," the broadcaster announced, "officials are reminding people of the panic surrounding the War of the Worlds broadcast of 1939 with Orson Welles. Next news at midnight."

As soon as the news broadcast was finished, a Disc Jockey came on air.

"Well, you heard it," he said in a joking tone. "No Martians tonight. So right now I'd like to dedicate this song to the Emperor of Mars wherever he is."

Then a song poured from the radios, the soulful sound of The Great Pretender by a group called The Platters. In a wonderful bold voice the lead singer began, *"Oh, yes, I'm the Great Pretender"* as the background singers doo-wopped in complementing voices. None of the townspeople said anything as the music drifted across the tracks and across the field. They seemed to be still waiting for something. But nothing came.

Matthew was still in shock. More so than Bernie who once again simply shrugged. And more than Nicodemus who sat still and looked straight ahead.

One by one, the townspeople began to leave, mostly in silence and disappointment.

"Matthew," Bernie said.

Matthew turned around to see Bernie stand up and move to the edge of the landing pad. "I'm gonna go, okay?" Matthew's eyes fell to Nancy who stood waiting for Bernie.

"I'm gonna ask Nancy to my place to watch TV," Bernie said, "It's still not too late to catch some shows."

He picked up his BB gun and walked to the edge of the landing pad.

Bernie was leaving and it didn't sit well with Matthew. He didn't mind if some of the townspeople left, but not Bernie. Bernie was part of the team that would be meeting the Emperor of Mars. Bernie couldn't leave, not yet.

"He's gonna come," Matthew said desperately. "All that meant was that he isn't coming anywhere else. He's coming here."

Bernie shrugged in his usual manner, "Yeah, maybe. But I wanna watch TV. So does Nancy." He stepped down to the ground where Nancy stood waiting.

"Then go ahead. I don't care."

Bernie knew the tone of Matthew's voice, he wanted to stay but he wanted to go more.

"Matthew," Bernie said, "he's not coming."

Matthew's disappointment was all too obvious. Bernie and Nancy walked back past the elevators and towards Main Street.

"The Emperor is gonna come and nobody but me is gonna see him," shouted Matthew.

The Anderson family exchanged looks and finally Anderson stood up and turned to Nicodemus still sitting in his chair and staring at the circle in the field. Anderson nodded to Nicodemus who didn't notice and then helped his wife up. Dolores joined them and they walked towards their truck.

Matthew was standing very still now as his mind raced through a series of thoughts. This couldn't be happening he thought, this had to be a mistake, the Emperor was coming here. All the signs pointed to it. The crop circle, Thunder Hill, Nicodemus.

Matthew, in his turmoil, had forgotten about Nicodemus.

Nicodemus hadn't really noticed much after the announcement on the radio. Like it happened in the past his memory had flashes of moments but nothing that really formulated long enough to mean anything. It was like he was watching two-second segments of his life on the screen.

He had these visions in the past but never with so much frequency as they revealed things he hadn't thought about for years. Things he had forgotten.

One of the flashes was a moment on Thunder Hill as a building was burning. And then what looked like a lightning bolt that seared from the sky dividing into six separate lightning bolts, each of which blasted into the ground illuminating, for a second, the main street of the town and strange grey forms that resembled shadow-like figures that moved across the street.

"Nicodemus!" a voice cried in the night. "Nicodemus". And Nicodemus, in his dream, felt someone pulling his arm.

"Nicodemus," Matthew shouted as he pushed against Nicodemus's arm. Nicodemus snapped back to the reality of the landing pad. He turned to look at Matthew.

"He is coming, I know he is, and so do you, Nicodemus," Matthew said in what was more like a plea than a statement.

"Maybe not," was all that Nicodemus could say.

"He's supposed to come. He said he would. He's supposed to be here, Damn it."

Matthew kicked his chair off the landing pad when suddenly he felt Nicodemus' strong arm grip him. Matthew reacted by swinging at Nicodemus, a harmless maneuver even if the intent was real. Nicodemus held onto Matthew to protect the boy from falling.

"Let me go!" Matthew yelled, "You don't care, you made me believe, you said he was coming."

Nicodemus gripped Matthew enough to contain him and knelt down, "Matthew, you listen to me. I didn't tell you nothing about the

Emperor of Mars. Nothing. You come around, wanna help me do this and that, I said okay. Fact is, I liked the company. But your daddy isn't coming back, he's never coming back. And you got to take that for a fact."

Matthew calmed down for a moment but his eyes burned with anger and disappointment.

"I'm sorry, boy, I'm truly sorry for you," Nicodemus continued, surprised at the clarity of his thoughts. It was as if something was freed from within him, some demon that held him back for so many years.

"If there was anything I could do, I would," Nicodemus said, "But you got your mom and your grandma and your life is with them. You gotta just accept that."

"But I miss him," Matthew said quietly, "At least I think I miss him. I don't even know."

"Everyone misses someone who left them," Nicodemus said. "It ain't special to you. And I ain't gonna tell ya you shouldn't miss him because that's your daddy. But you can find a place to put him where he'll always be."

"Where?" asked Matthew.

Nicodemus pointed to his own heart, "Right here in that very part of you that gives life. You remember him here every day of your living life."

"I don't get it," was all Matthew could say.

"You will. Look at you, good-looking man. One of these days, some pretty girl's gonna catch you and first thing you get to be a daddy of your own. That's the way this life works."

Matthew eyes glistened. He looked at Nicodemus who now had taken his grip off Matthew's arms. Free now and still unsure Matthew backed away until he reached the end of the landing pad. Then he jumped off and ran leaving Nicodemus alone.

"He's a boy," a voice spoke behind Nicodemus. He turned to see Miss Major. "Did you have to be so hard on him?"

"Truth is hard sometimes. Better he knows now."

"All of this, about space beings, why did you start this?"

"I didn't start it."

"Then who are you waiting for?" She asked. Then, as if to answer her, Nicodemus turned to the photograph of Mary. Miss Major followed his look. "Did you believe someone was coming from out there?" she said carefully, not wanting to upset him. "Was it the war, did it change you that much?"

Nicodemus looked back at her and again, his world became clear.

"I'm not crazy, even though everyone in town thinks I am."

"I don't think you're crazy," she said.

Then came a precious moment of silence, they both knew the loneliness each other felt even if they were different ages and had different lives. For that moment they were one. And neither knew what to do next. But they didn't have to wait long.

On her way back to the truck, Mrs. Anderson had an odd feeling that caused her to look up at the elevator and the Christmas lights that ran all the way up to the top. And that was when she saw something else. She stopped in her tracks, causing Anderson and Dolores to turn back at her.

"Look! There!" Mrs. Anderson said. Anderson followed her look, then Dolores. They both strained their necks to look up towards the top of the elevator.

And they saw what she saw.

33

It took Matthew a few seconds to see what the Andersons were seeing. It was something that seemed to be suspended in the air, floating near the top of one of the elevators. The object had a silvery, translucent form that seemed to tremble as it floated.

Some of the townspeople stopped in their tracks and looked up. Others ran away and still others jumped into their trucks and cars. The Reverend stood still watching like the others around him. His expression grew strong and firm and he was not about to believe in what he saw.

Elana had just arrived when she heard the crowd talking and pointing upwards. She also saw the shiny silver object as the Christmas lights on the elevator revealed its shape which to her looked almost like a white sheet fluttering in the wind on a clothesline.

Bernie and Nancy saw it also. They were both silent until Bernie found the words.

"Oh boy," he said nervously. Then he raised his BB gun.

Above the crowd a good hundred feet, the object undulated back and forth. It was at least twenty feet long and moving closer to the elevator.

"It's headed for the elevator!" Somebody shouted from the crowd.

Anderson shouted, "Damn thing's gonna hit it!"

The object bumped softly into the top of the elevator and some of its translucent skin ripped and sailed gently down falling like a leaf.

A thought struck Matthew, something odd and familiar. And in the next instant he knew what it was.

"Tommy," he whispered. Then he looked at Nicodemus again and said it louder, "Tommy!"

As the silvery shape turned it revealed a makeshift basket tied to a weather balloon. The same weather balloon hanging in Simpson's store. But all was not going well as Tommy was now desperately trying to steer away from the elevator and the Christmas lights. It had taken him a good two hours to fill the balloon with helium and even a slight rip into the balloon could easily cause a fire and at the worst, an explosion.

His big hoax was turning into a potential disaster.

Looking down nearly ten stories Tommy desperately tried to figure out what to do now. But the balloon nudged into the side of the elevator and back and a strong wind pushed him towards the Christmas lights. The balloon bumped hard into the elevator and hit the Christmas lights strong enough to knock them against the building's side. All it took was one tiny red bulb to crack and the electrical spark to arc across three inches towards the balloon which had suffered a thin rip and which in turn caused the helium to hiss out.

Flame erupted instantly as the fire inhaled the helium and two thin streams of flame dripped down towards the ground.

"They're shooting at us!" someone yelled, "They're trying to kill us!"

Panic ensued on the ground, people ran for cover. Elana turned to look for Matthew but only saw Nicodemus in the panic-stricken crowd.

Nicodemus was running towards the elevator and she knew Matthew would be somewhere near him.

Miss Major found herself guiding people to safety, pointing directions to clear areas as the crowd dispersed. Elana approached Nicodemus and saw that Matthew was already there.

"It's Tommy Simpson, Nicodemus," Matthew shouted as he stood up on the platform, "he's up there."

Nicodemus looked up, his mind racing for a strategy. He knew that if the fire caught the flammable grain dust, the whole elevator could go up. Maybe even both of them. And fire could spread to the town.

"Damn fool," was all he could say. Then he broke into a run to the elevator and entered the wide scale door, disappearing inside.

"Nicodemus!" Matthew shouted as Bernie appeared at his side.

"That fire's gonna spread to the wheat," Bernie said. "The whole elevator's gonna go up."

Matthew stared ahead, "I gotta help him."

"You can't go, Matthew, you're a kid," Bernie said.

"I gotta," Matthew said as he moved toward the elevator.

"Matthew!" Bernie pleaded. But he was already running up to the elevator doors as Bernie stood there. Then Matthew went inside. Elana appeared as did Miss Major.

"Where is Matthew, Bernie?" Elana said.

Bernie, unsure of whether to tell or not, hesitated.

"Bernie, where is Matthew?" Elena and Bernie turned to see Miss Major who now stood beside them.

"He's gone inside", Bernie managed to say, "inside!"

Elana and Miss Major both reacted.

"Oh God," was all Elana could say.

Suddenly shouts from the crowd made them turn their heads upward where they could barely see Tommy and the balloon dangling dangerously close to the elevator.

With the balloon almost gone Tommy had managed to throw a rope that hooked onto an inspection walkway that led across the top of the elevator toward a doorway. The rope kept the basket from falling but fire was already creeping up towards Tommy.

Realizing he had only one chance Tommy leaped onto the walkway nearly falling and having to drag himself up onto it. He stood and looked down at the townspeople below. Suddenly the basket fell against the elevator and lodged itself into a tight corner as the fire began to spread to onto the wood siding. Tommy was now trapped as the fire began to burn below him.

Meanwhile, inside the elevator, Nicodemus pulled off a fire extinguisher and ran to the passenger lift that normally carried workmen to the top of the grain elevator for maintenance or routine safety checks. He climbed in and pulled the lever and the lift clunked and jerked and then slowly lifted upwards in the narrow shaft that rose all ten stories to the top.

Matthew arrived just in time to see the lift rise to the floor above.

"Nicodemus!" He yelled, "It's on fire!"

His words went unheard as the lift disappeared on its journey to the top of the building. Matthew ran to the wooden stairway that wound upwards alongside the lift shaft. It was the only way and Matthew did not hesitate as he began to climb the stairs, passing through a Dickensian labyrinth of wood frames and iron gears.

At the firehall Anderson and Lorne had already begun the fire alarm and as they backed out with the truck the volunteer firemen came running. Anderson greeted them as they approached.

"It's not a spaceship. It's a fire! With all that grain inside, that place will go up like an Atomic Bomb," he said as the men leaped onto the truck and turned it towards Main Street.

34

When the fire alarm shattered the silence of Simpson's living room, the reaction was instant. Mrs. Simpson and Stephanie were startled but said nothing as Simpson rose and looked out the window. He didn't need to figure it out as he looked in the night sky, now illuminated by the fire.

"The elevators," he said to himself. And then he ran to the door leaving them sitting. Stephanie waited for a long moment after she heard the back door slam before she said anything.

"Mom, what's happening?"

Mrs. Simpson waited for a thought to clear her mind, then she smiled, "It's all right, sweetheart. Everything is fine."

But Stephanie knew that everything was not fine. And she knew Matthew was out there.

At the top of the elevator Tommy had made it onto the walkway but flames already were licking their way toward him. His only route now was to enter the elevator through the door in front of him. In the moment he made his decision, his mind raced back to when he had sneaked out of his home to go to his father's store.

He had always wanted to do something with the weather balloon that his father had bought on one of his surplus trips, where he picked up used army goods that he could resell to farmers and hunters in Empire. The balloon had attachments that would accommodate a basket under it. Tommy had read that sometimes military people would put animals and even dummies in these baskets.

That became his inspiration, the biggest joke of his life to date, and on the entire town. His joke on Matthew had worked very well and this was the next logical stage. But it didn't work out that way. Now he was standing ten stories above the ground with fire lapping towards him with the heat becoming more intense as the fire grew.

Tommy reached for the door handle. It didn't turn. He turned it hard, harder, but again it didn't open. Tommy realized it was locked from the inside. In the same instant, the door suddenly burst open and Tommy stepped away, fearing fire.

Instead, Nicodemus appeared, holding the fire extinguisher.

"Come here you fool kid," Nicodemus shouted. Tommy stepped back until he could feel the heat of the fire. Nicodemus stepped out and grabbed him by the shirt and pulled him inside.

"Leave me alone," Tommy whimpered.

"Shut up," was all Nicodemus said as he pulled the boy inside. He slammed the door shut but smoke was already spiraling upwards from under the door.

"It was just a joke," he shouted.

"Some joke," Nicodemus said as he pushed Tommy back towards the lift. Just then an explosion rocked the entire elevator from above and the support beams above the lift suddenly lurched and tilted. The lift jolted up and down with a sickening metal grating sound. Nicodemus stepped onto it and turned the lever but nothing happened. The lift wasn't working anymore.

"The steps," Nicodemus pointed and he pushed Tommy to the stairs heading down. The smoke was thicker as they ran down the wooden steps to the next level below. With luck the fire might not have reached this level yet, Nicodemus figured.

Outside, the explosion looked more like fireworks as white sparks shot out from the top of the elevator. The fire engine had arrived and as they began to pull out the hoses they realized something.

"It's too high up," Lorne shouted, "We can't reach it." Standing safely away, Bernie watched the fire with fear and apprehension. Miss Major was there also and she held Elana who cried as she watched.

"Matthew, please God, help him!" Elana cried.

Matthew had made it nearly halfway up the steps until the explosion had blown out the stairs above him. Now he looked for another way up. But first he looked down at the elevator shaft that ran down at least seventy feet. It was dark and ominous and when flame flickered below he made out cables that crisscrossed wood beams and iron grids and scoops that lifted the grain that now took on a monstrous look.

"Matthew!" came the shout that turned his head. He looked up where the stairs had collapsed and saw Nicodemus and Tommy. They were about fifteen feet above him on the edge of the other end of the stairs with an open gap between floors.

"Get outta here," Nicodemus shouted. "Go back down."

Matthew stood there. Then he spoke.

"Jump!"

"No," Nicodemus yelled louder. "Get going. Leave! Get outta here!"

"It's your only chance," Matthew said again, "You gotta jump. Now!"

"You crazy kid, why don't you listen to me?" Nicodemus shouted as he pulled Tommy towards the last step which suddenly fell away with nothing but empty space between them and Matthew two floors down.

"I came to get you, you're my friend," Matthew said.

Another fireball of combustible dust rocked the building. Nicodemus grabbed Tommy by the arm. "I'm going to lower you as far as I can," he said, "Then you'll have to jump." Tommy shook his head, "No, I can't, I can't do it."

"You will," Nicodemus said as he swung Tommy out into the open space. Tommy closed his eyes, gripping onto Nicodemus. "Jump!" said Nicodemus as he let go of Tommy. Tommy screamed as he fell towards Matthew. When he hit solid wood again, Matthew grabbed him and pulled him back.

"Get back," shouted Nicodemus.

Matthew stepped back as Nicodemus then jumped down. He came down hard, landing on his side. A shot of pain hot burned in his leg as he stood up.

"Nicodemus," Matthew said urgently. "Look".

Beneath them fire had now blocked the steps. There was no way to get down. Nicodemus stood up and the pain jabbed at his leg making him almost collapse. Matthew noticed it immediately.

"You're hurt," Matthew said.

"No time for that," Nicodemus said as his mind raced for an escape. Suddenly Tommy bolted and ran towards the open lift shaft. But Nicodemus leapt forward and grabbed him just before Tommy would have stepped off and fallen several stories down. But Nicodemus's weak leg collapsed and Tommy fell to the wood floor hitting his head. He lay perfectly still. Matthew ran over as Nicodemus bent over Tommy.

"What happened," Matthew asked.

"Unconscious," Nicodemus answered, "Fool kid knocked himself out." Fighting the pain in his leg, Nicodemus bent down and lifted Tommy, the extra weight searing more pain into his damaged leg.

"What are we gonna do?" Matthew shouted.

Nicodemus looked in all directions. There was fire above and fire below and smoke everywhere else. Then he looked at the lift shaft. Images began to flash in his head, images of combat, images of Thunder Hill and fire and then sharp angled lights that flashed like diamonds. He seemed in a daze as he stood there perfectly still.

Matthew realized Nicodemus was falling into that frightening state he had seen him like before. And it scared him even more.

"Nicodemus, you can't go away in your head, not now," Matthew begged. "We need you, both of us, we need you!"

Matthew would remember what happened next for the rest of his life. He would remember it as clear as the wide open blue skies of the prairies. He would remember it forever. And the last thing he would remember is what he said.

"Nicodemus!"

As the heat from the fires above and below them became hotter and beams began to crack and smoke filled the floor something happened like Matthew had never seen. Like nobody in Empire or maybe even the whole world had ever seen.

Something impossible.

35

It began when the smoke got so thick that Matthew and Nicodemus could barely see each other. It choked at their throats and the heat from the fires burned against their clothes. Matthew's eyesight began to blur as he and Nicodemus carried Tommy and stumbled towards the only open space left. The lift shaft. All Matthew knew was that if they jumped they would never survive what would be a seven story fall.

It was then that Matthew felt a blast of cool air drift past him. It was like someone had opened a window and fresh air was blowing in. But there were no windows here. And then the light came. It was soft at first, streaming through the smoke in narrow shafts like arrows shooting down at an angle, bouncing off the wood floors. When Matthew turned to Nicodemus he saw the light shards bouncing off his shoulders, embracing him with fingers of luminous radiance that seemed to look like thin small grey beings. Like the shadows Nicodemus had seen before. He held the unconscious Tommy in his arms and stood still as he was covered in a brilliant glow.

Matthew didn't know what to think. Was he dying, was this what happened when someone died. But he could still feel the cool air that by now had pushed away the heat of the flames which now were flickering dangerously close to all three.

"Matthew, come here," a voice said. But Matthew didn't know who said it. It sounded like Nicodemus but he was looking straight at Nicodemus and he wasn't saying a word. "Come here," it said again. Matthew looked again at Nicodemus. "Come here now," Nicodemus's voice said, even though his mouth did not move.

Matthew walked slowly, entering the luminous light that spilled around him now, covering him in a cool soft surface. Nicodemus looked down at him and smiled.

Then, a magical thing happened. Nicodemus began to rise while still holding Tommy. Crystal-like flashes of blue light enveloped the three of them. Matthew looked down and saw the floor cracking and groaning as the fire ate away underneath it. Finally the floor began to buckle and cave and then it collapsed completely.

But Matthew, Nicodemus and Tommy were still there, floating in mid air.

This was impossible, people didn't float. Matthew clutched at Nicodemus's shoulder as he looked ahead. Where the lift shaft was a rainbow of magnificent colors began to form creating a spiral tunnel through the smoke and fire. A glass-like tunnel that led down to the ground floor.

Now Matthew felt himself moving. He realized that the three of them were slowly floated toward the tunnel which was wide enough for all of them to fit. All around the fire raged and wood beams collapsed. But nothing seemed to be able to break through the opaque tunnel as the three of them floated down the shaft, passing each floor on their way down. Matthew began to enjoy the feeling and his mind drifted until he remembered where he was. He glanced up at Nicodemus who held onto both boys now, looking straight ahead. "Are we dead?" Matthew thought. But just as soon as he did, Nicodemus's voice answered "No, we're not dead."

When Matthew looked at Nicodemus again everything began to darken. Soon the fire was way above them but they continued to fall slowly. Matthew's mind began to get hazy and his vision began to blur again. That was when he felt Nicodemus let go of him and Tommy. Matthew looked up again long enough to see Nicodemus smile at him before Matthew's world turned to black. And he clearly heard Nicodemus speak even though his mouth never moved.

"They're here, Matthew, they're all here, I'll see you again. I promise." There was another flash of brilliant light again and Matthew looked down to see the main floor coming up at him. He shouted and then lost consciousness.

Outside a rain of blue light beams shot up and out of the elevator into the night sky, moving like lightning straight up until they disappeared. Miss Major was one of a handful of people who saw it. A beam of light shot up from the burning elevator and into the night sky and then was gone. It happened so fast that she wasn't sure if she saw anything at all. In later years she remembered it less and less until it became lost in the memories of a distant time.

The sounds of breaking wood and voices faded in and out of Matthew's head. When he opened his eyes he was looking at his mother. Then Miss Major appeared beside her and they were both talking to him but Matthew couldn't hear what they were saying. But he could see that it was still night and he was outside on the grass. Then he went to sleep again.

36

When Matthew awoke he was looking into blinding light. At first he thought it was the magical light he had seen. That led to the memory of what had happened to him and Tommy and Nicodemus. But it now seemed more like a dream. It took a minute to adjust his eyes to the light that he now realized was coming from his bedroom window.

"Matthew," Elana's soft voice spoke.

Matthew nodded as though to confirm that. Yes, he was Matthew. But he didn't remember how he got here.

All he remembered was the elevator and the fire and then the light. And then the other part of his memory came back. He was floating or flying and he and Nicodemus and Tommy were descending down the lift shaft as though they rested on a pillow of air being gently lowered. And the heat was gone. He remembered Nicodemus's face and the words he spoke without actually speaking.

"They're here," Nicodemus's voice now echoed. They're here, thought Matthew.

Who was here?

Elana handed him some cards. He raised them to eye level. There was a card from the Grade 6 class and one from Stephanie and there was another one. It had one of those French paintings on the front. Matthew knew who that was from and he eagerly opened it. There, under the pre-printed greeting was her name. And even better she had personally written her own message. "To the bravest person I've ever known, get better soon." It was signed, "Love, Jenny Major."

Jenny? Who was Jenny? It took him a few seconds to realize she had signed the card with her first name. The card became intensely personal and he would keep it for the rest of his life.

"Jenny," Matthew said softly.

Matthew stayed in bed the whole day and Elana brought him some new comic books that she had bought with her own money.

Somehow, she seemed to be happier than she usually was. He had even heard her sing to herself. Babka of course, kept praying as she always did. But somehow, the house seemed a little brighter.

That night Miss Major walked alone to where the elevator stood. It was gone now, just a pile of blackened metal and smoldering wood beams.

The other elevator had narrowly missed catching fire. She walked to Nicodemus's house and stood there for awhile as though waiting for him to step outside. But nobody stepped out. She had found the photograph of his wife now in a broken frame. Miss Major picked it up, looked at it, and set it down on the porch where Nicodemus's dog sat alone. She finally turned and walked away.

Miss Major became different after that night and stayed in Empire for another year but then left. By the time Matthew was in high school, he got a postcard from Paris, it was from Miss Major. All she said was "you were right, it wasn't as far away as Mars after all". She signed it, "Hope you remember me, love, Jenny". Remember her? Matthew would always remember her.

On the third night after the fire, Matthew found himself standing on the landing pad. Someone had taken the opportunity to pirate some of the wood and the firepots were all gone. But the crop circle remained. In years to come, nothing could grow within the circle again.

With the passing of three days Matthew still couldn't explain what really happened that night. Tommy didn't remember anything at all. Strangely enough, after that, he became a nicer kid and years after Matthew would meet him at a Midas Muffler shop and learned he had become a teacher himself.

Matthew turned towards Nicodemus's house where the dog sat and waited. He too waited for the door to open and for Nicodemus to step out with a hammer or a saw in his hand ready to work.

But he didn't step out. Nobody saw Nicodemus again. Some of the people had said he died in the fire but Matthew knew he didn't. He had seen Nicodemus, he was in that magic light and he heard Nicodemus say they had come for him. He didn't know who they were but somehow Matthew knew Nicodemus was going home. And besides that, there was no trace of him anywhere.

Matthew had overheard the doctor had told Elana that he had some smoke inhalation and that he had probably hallucinated whatever memories he had of Nicodemus. But Matthew remembered very clearly how they all got out, all three of them. And he knew he wasn't seeing things. Because he was there.

Picking up the photograph of Mary, Matthew walked inside Nicodemus's home. The furniture was still in place. Nobody had ransacked it yet. He looked around but the house was now nothing more than wood and frames. There was no life here.

He stepped out into the evening and looked up at the night sky. "Come back, Nicodemus," he said softly and waited for the answer. And then, as if to answer, a dust devil whirled past him and spun its way off into the darkness and was gone. The dog shivered a slight bit. Above them Venus had made its usual appearance and then, in the part of the night sky where Mars should be, Matthew saw a sparkle. Then another. Two in a row. Maybe, just maybe...

"Hi, Matthew," a familiar voice said behind him.

Matthew turned to face Stephanie, who walked up to him.

"Everybody knows about you. You were very brave."

"Yeah," Matthew answered with a shrug of his shoulders.

"It's real sad about Nicodemus."

"He's not dead."

Stephanie nodded and then Matthew turned and began to walk away from her. But this time

Stephanie would have none of it. She had been practicing the now for the last two days. And she wasn't going to let it go to waste.

"Matthew," Stephanie said with an unusual firmness. Matthew turned to her again.

"Matthew, I liked you since the first grade and you like me, I know you did because I just know but I'm not gonna chase you anymore." Then Stephanie whirled around and started walking away from him. Matthew watched her with a surprised look. This time he felt differently about dismissing her. This time she walked away from him. Maybe she would understand what happened. Maybe it took kids to believe some things.

"Stephanie."

Stephanie kept walking. Matthew finally had to run to catch up to her. As he matched her stride Stephanie kept walking and avoiding his look.

"Stephanie."

She finally stopped and glared at him. "I mean it this time," she said with the same resolve, "Glenn Kristy came with me and my mom to the movies twice already." There was a moment of silence as both of them stood there. A chill had come with the darkness and Stephanie shivered a little. Matthew had never really looked at her like he was now. She was pretty and had a sparkle about her that he couldn't quite explain. Something had changed in her, and Matthew realized she wasn't just some girl anymore. She was different and he was glad he ran after her. And he even surprised her when he spoke.

"I was thinking," Matthew stumbled, "Maybe we could go to the movie. I mean, if Glenn isn't taking you."

"Me and you? Just the two of us?

"It's the Natalie Wood movie tonight," he said, then remembered, "You kinda look like her."

"It's adult."

Matthew had the answer, "Maybe with all the excitement, nobody will notice two kids."

Stephanie smiled. She had taken a risk, but it seemed like it was all working out. She needed one more move. "I'll buy popcorn," she said and waited a second, "If we share."

Matthew nodded, "Okay."

They both started walking. After a few steps Stephanie casually reached for Matthew's hand. He resisted but after a few more tries on her part, he took her hand in his. It felt warm and good and for the first time he had felt a happiness that was different than what he was used to. He liked that Stephanie cared about him and he liked that he cared about her.

As they walked away from Nicodemus's house and the crop circle and the ruins of the elevator Matthew knew he never did get some of the answers he wanted. But maybe nobody did, he thought. Maybe, like the crop circle in the field, things just happen. The dog slowly rose and followed the two of them.

And Matthew figured that Miss Major was right about something. There was a whole future for him to face beginning tomorrow. He had read something in a magazine that said people would be in space and Matthew wanted to see that.

But whatever else he expected, he hoped he'd see Nicodemus again someday before he got old and died like the people Babka prayed for. Somehow, Matthew thought, he was about as close to the Emperor of Mars that he could hope for. And if the Emperor couldn't come to him, then maybe Matthew might have to come to the Emperor. But that would be a long time from now. Right now he was going to a movie like he did so many other times but with one major change. This time it was with Stephanie.

As the pair walked down Main Street to towards the lights of the theater, the little town of Empire set in for another quiet and peaceful night. Above, stars twinkled in the endless darkness of space and for the first time anyone could remember, the red planet, Mars, shone brighter than any of them.

3773011R00164

Made in the USA
San Bernardino, CA
26 August 2013